G000254405

COTSWOLD VILLAGES

THE VILLAGE SERIES

Yorkshire Villages
G. Bernard Wood

Surrey Villages
Derek Pitt and Michael Shaw

Suffolk Villages
Allan Jobson

Devon Villages
S. H. Burton

Cotswold Villages

JUNE R. LEWIS

ROBERT HALE · LONDON

ISBN 0 7091 4311 7

Robert Hale & Company
63 Old Brompton Road
London, S.W.7

PRINTED IN GREAT BRITAIN BY
CLARKE, DOBLE & BRENDON LTD.
PLYMOUTH

Contents

Illustrations

Wyck Rissington—a farmer's tombstone
Gustav Holst's house on Wyck Rissington common
Lunchtime for the woodmen at Farmington Grove
Peter and Joy Evans, furniture maker and woodcarver

Between pages 80 and 81

Children's singing games performed annually at Little Rissington
Maypole dancing by pupils of Ampney Crucis school
George Swinford at his Filkins 'studio'
Chartist bungalow at Minster Lovell
A school group from Solihull at work on a practical maths lesson at
    Burford Wild Life Park
Tree planting to mark Meyseyhampton's school centenary
Nags Head hamlet in the Stroud Valley

Between pages 96 and 97

Donnington Brewery on the Dikler
Young anglers at Lower Slaughter mill
Widford's ancient church stands alone in a field
Double row of beakheads arched over Windrush church door
Sheephill Barn on the Roman Akeman Road
Barn at Naunton
Mr Stallworthy, one of Cotswold's last millers
Keble Bridge links the Eastleaches

Between pages 112 and 113

Bibury—with Arlington Mill across the bridge
The Leach makes one of its brief winter appearances
The charming Coln from Coln St Aldwyn Hill
Patricia Haines spinning
Theo Merrett, leatherworker of Far Oakridge
David White thatching
Tump Cottage at Barrow
The Waterley Bottom Mummers

Between pages 128 and 129

Laurie Lee's childhood home in the Slad Valley
Farmstead seen from Painswick Beacon
Sunset over South Cerney water
That other Paradise—near Cranham
Hatherop's tricycling tramp

The photograph showing Peter Juggins at Fairford church
was supplied by Wiltshire Newspapers; those of David
White thatching Tump Cottage by A. G. G. Hurcombe of
Gretton. All the others were taken by the author.

MAP   *pages 16–17*

Acknowledgements

Particular mention must be made of:

The Bodleian Library, Oxford, Gloucestershire Records Office and The Staff of Bingham Library, Cirencester for allowing me facilities for research.

Mr A. G. Hurcombe and the Wiltshire Newspapers for scaling wobbly ladders, to which I have an aversion, in order to supply me with the three photographs mentioned.

Capt. R. C. G. Vivian, (Clerk of the Course, Salisbury) for information on the origins of Bibury Race Club.

The Editor of *Cotswold Life* for permission to include parts of features which have been written by me for that magazine.

To my innumerable Cotswold friends, in particular, Mike Hart who has interpreted parts of the geology with me; Richard Chidlaw, Father Christmas of the Waterley Bottom Mummers, whose fund of stories could only be dipped into, George Swinford of Filkins and Peter Juggins of Chedworth and a whole host of craftsmen; to all Cotsallers, peer and poet, the titled and the tramp who have entertained me in their castles and cottages and shepherd's hut and to the memory of Pop, a true son of Cotswold —thank you.

FOR NEN
IN
LOVE AND GRATITUDE

Introduction

I T is man's ability to work with nature that makes the Cotswolds a special area, one could almost say the heart of England itself, for here the Cotsaller shaped the stone from under his feet to raise a roof over his head. It is this, above all, that makes Cotswold architecture so domestic, and yet grand; imposing and venerable through its very affinity to the landscape from which it was born, and it is the villages nestling in the folds of the hills that hold the secret of what is Cotswold so that the heart of every Englishman beats that little bit faster as though one had said 'home'.

Our urban cousins smile at Hodge in the Cotswold pub and imitate his long vowels and slow speech, he is part of the country scene and they have seen his like on their television screens. Hodge, however, aware or unaware of their amusement endures their company with a quiet dignity, he knows that they are unlikely to be his neighbour. Country life is a great equalizer.

The Cotswold village which has bred peer and peasant, poet and painter, jockey and show-jumper, the famous and the infamous, home of Iron Age man and base of Concorde, attracting the antiquary, archaeologist, aviator, and speculator, has become the estate agent's greatest hunting ground.

Derelict cottages are snapped up, converted and glorified out of all recognition inside. Woe betide the 'gin and Jaguar' types, however, who have their Cotswold cottage as a status symbol, if they tinker about with the externals. Hodge will be there at the Council offices, mud on his boots and fire in his heart. He may not be able to afford a 'cot' in his own village but he'll take good care that no-one wipes out the character lines of it with an alien hand.

To the visitor the villages may be clusters of homely cottages around a Norman or Saxon church with perhaps an imposing Manor house, a reminder of feudalism, steeped in history and standing in its own grounds. To the native they are home, their pattern as accepted as that of night and day.

To these who come upon our villages by way of devious narrow lanes and the spirit of the wanderer on a summer Sunday drive they present the idyllic picture of country life, somnolent and safe in their sober stone solidity. But as with an Old Master, irreplaceable and inimitable in design and execution, they age gracefully with no sign of the labour, torment and tears that went into composing such pictures.

Unlike the portrait caught in paint against canvas, the village picture is not static, within those solid stone settings and against the rolling hills, nebulous to the eye, solid underfoot, are the folks who made, and still make, the Cotswold villages the heart of England. It is they who have expended their lives and love in the making of such national heritages.

And it is people who are more important than monuments. All too often we revere a building or a work of art with little thought of the men who made it so, which is rather like worshipping Sunday instead of God.

I

The Ancient Cotswold Ridgeway

TORMARTON TO EDGE

GENESIS becomes geological fact in the formation of Cotswold country. When the waters gathered together unto one place and the dry land appeared, the hard Palaeozoic rocks of the Welsh borderlands and the oolitic limestone of the Cotswolds parted to let the low-lying Severn Vale run its own distinctive course to the seaways.

Hard as it is, the great oolitic limestone has not been so resistant to erosion as its older neighbour across the Vale, or that venerable ancient, the Malverns.

Time and clime have pushed the escarpment eastwards, and in consequence, remnants of Cotswold have been left behind: the 'outliers'—Robins Wood Hill, Churchdown Hill and Bredon Hill—lie as dropped toys in the Vale below; and the inflowing tide has no easy passage as it rushes up the Severn. Cotswold has its foot out to trip the Atlantic surge, for it is the hard limestone bands in the clays of the river bed which give rise to the phenomenon the Severn Bore: Cotswold is not easily erased from the scene.

It is along the rather ragged edge of the escarpment which was so dramatically rent asunder from the main mass of rocks millions of years ago that civilization took its first questing steps as man discovered what Cotswold country had to offer. The dust of ages has long since settled on this ancient ridgeway where the going was safer than in the water-logged valleys, forest and scrub of the claylands below. The tracks made in the springy turf by animal and man are now sealed to the earth by metalled roads along which motorists speed, but we shall slow down often on our way to meet again the Cotsallers who knew this land before us, and to see what we have all made of Cotswold.

Palaeolithic man left little trace of his being. What fragments have been found along with those of the woolly rhinoceros and elephant have been very few indeed and on the gravel terraces below, having little chance of surviving the ravages of the later ice-ages.

It is to the old Britons who succeeded them about 2000 B.C. that we must turn if we are to look for the village life of our hills.

The early Britons probably came inland by way of the Bristol Channel, on which the trade of the west still ebbs and flows, and quickly sought a way on to the high ground which then, as now, makes an impressive sweep against the skyline. One has to admire the temerity with which the neolithic immigrants found their way through the dense alien woodlands. That they liked what they found speaks to us in the shape of their long barrows which accentuate the prominent features of the Cotswold landscape. And tumuli hereabouts say that here they stayed—never again to feel the warmth of the Mediterranean of whose stock they sprang.

When we talk of the Cotswold ridgeway it is generally of that great trackway which was the main artery of communication running from the Bristol waterway to the Humber, so we shall travel along it here and there as we go northwards but for the purpose of seeking out the villages we shall often stray from it. Authorities define the thoroughfare as climbing the Lansdown plateau at Bath, into Gloucestershire by Cold Ashton, alongside the hill-fort at Little Sodbury, north-east to Chavenage Green, along the top of the Duntisbourne valley and across to Birdlip. From there is crossed the Coln at Andoversford and the Windrush at Naunton, through Stow-on-the-Wold to leave the hills just after Adlestrop.

But it is along the ragged edge of the Cotswolds that we shall make our way for the scarp is studded with antiquities: long barrows and round barrows and Iron-Age forts.

As there was no accepted trackway for traversing the wolds in the beginning it would be on the highest ground that the early Briton made his home. The ridgeway came into being as a result of his trading with the flint workers in Wiltshire. And yet the spirit of the ancient road lingers yet as the long walled lanes takes us across windswept fields to Tormarton where the Normans raised a church.

Yate once lay beneath a fine veil of silky dust like the Sleeping Beauty's castle. But Yate did not slumber—although Alexander Staples has since 1590, so his epitaph tells us, and intends to until "the trumpet shall sound taratantara" and his mortal limbs "be joined to his spirit again". The quarrying activities which the discovery of celestine brought in its wake may have had no rousing effect on the sleeping father of eleven but it brought scientists to the strata and industry to the area. It is still the only area in England where it is mined, but the resources near Yate have been exhausted and the quarries eat along the north-west seam to Yate Court—and almost into Rangeworthy, veer north to Cromhall and out of the Cotswolds.

Now owned by the Bristol Mineral Co. whose twenty-five employees handle approximately 10,000 tons of celestine a year by mainly open-cast mining, the mineral which is hand-selected with picks finds its market chiefly in the United States and European countries. It has been used in pyrotechnics for many years—so the brilliant magnificence of firework displays, or a lone sailor's distress signal, may have started life at the foot of our hills. The old mills at Goose Green are still very much in use. About 25,000 tons of Greek magnestice and Italian marble chippings are ground here at the stone mills every year to provide us with talcum powder!

It is sometimes pleasant to deviate from the original track for good roads and curiosity lead the traveller on to Wickwar if only for the views it affords of the Cotswolds, and a glimpse at the medieval church, alone in a field and deserted by the village. The building character and style wear the border influence for here, too, it is varied. The small quarry is still active but the stone here is not that of the true oolite, but limestone nevertheless with a high PSV (polished stone value) so the rocks here are elevated no higher than the roads.

Tortworth farther west tempts anglers to its lakes, campanologists to the medieval bell in the church tower, and everyone to its famous old chestnut tree.

But we digress. It is time to return to the hills which we can do across Inglestone Common.

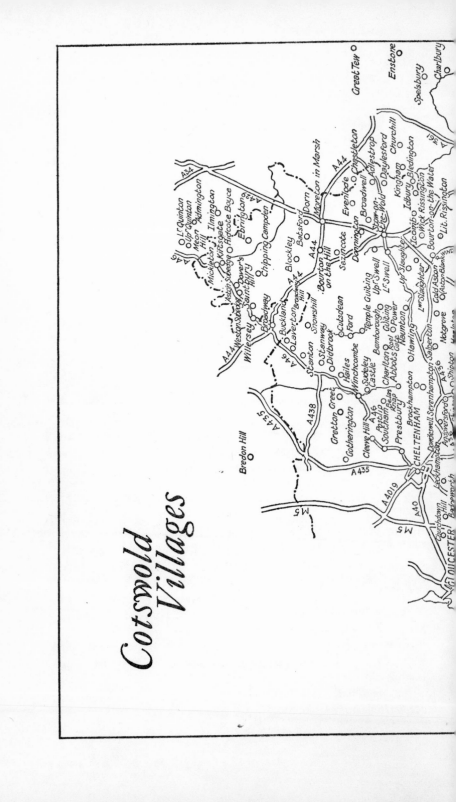

Cotswold
Villages

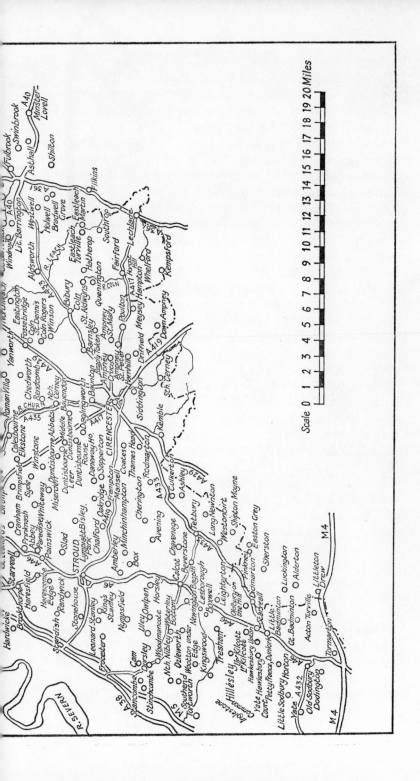

The friends of General Lord Robert Somerset built the tower at Hawkesbury Upton to elevate his memory and exercise the legs of pilgrims; for those who make the long winding climb do so for the magnificent views the tower affords rather than in homage to the distinguished General who fought at Waterloo. There are one hundred and forty-three steps to the top—an insignificant scrap of knowledge which we gathered under great stress as half-way down I was convulsed by a fit of giggles and obstructed our descent and others' ascent—for I could not help thinking of what might happen should we disagree on the total when we finally reached the bottom. We did. But as we contemplated on the value of such information and who should be entrusted (!) with the responsibility of a recount, Nen recalled taking two steps across each platform: so the majority agreed and a second climb was averted!

We will wait awhile here for those travellers who faithfully followed the acknowledged ridgeway, but like a hare one has to criss-cross the original track to see what Cotsallers have done away from its path.

From Old Sodbury a lane leads to Little Sodbury. The medieval church, where Tyndale was inspired to translate the Bible into English, huddles in ruins beneath ancient yews. The old church has furnished the new one with most of its stones, a chest, and a bell, and the devotees of Tyndale the panelled oak pulpit.

Grass-covered ramparts of the most notable of the Iron-Age earthworks make a distinctive plateau of some twelve acres where the ancients lived out their lives in a village of thatched huts.

Horton, set on a hill, is another quiet spot from which the traveller can take his bearings—on the east the valley of the Severn, on the west the steep Cotswold edge, and around him the foundations laid by the Normans at the church and the Court, to be followed later by the forerunner of enclosure by legislation when the seventeenth-century lords and tenants agreed to enclose part of the waste ground.

Close to the main road and overlooking the village is a hill-fort, the smoke from which would have been clearly visible from the one at Little Sodbury. Hawkesbury buildings have been refashioned since Saxon times and visitors to the church are requested to "leave their dogs at home and the women not to walk in with their pattens on".

I am sure that the Badmintons will lure many travellers to edge towards the east. We will quickly recall what they will have found as they left us at Tormarton.

Acton Turville's toll house will tell of other travellers who passed this way, many of whom must have lingered awhile at the old well in the centre of the village. Those that stayed were called to the old church by the bell in the antique turret, and baptized in the tub font which was rescued from ignominious service in a local farmyard. Old-fashioned roses tumble wantonly over the fences at the railway station, old boots and litter lie between the tracks. The coals in the pot-bellied stove in the waiting-room have long since died for no-one waits here any longer. The little station moulders away—it had its time of glory and importance and felt the tread of royal feet upon its platforms. Despite Acton Turville having accommodated the station the honour was accorded to Badminton without that village having the inconvenience of the noise and smoke: a measure of British Railway's business acumen before they abbreviated their lines and title as, for their own benefit, they ran special trains for the conveyance of spectators to the famous Three Day Event in addition to the normal daily runs to and from London, two up and three down.

One enters Great Badminton with respect. The buildings here are set out in a planned fashion and ducal coats of arms stare stonily down on the visitor from the walls on all sides of the neat and tidy streets. Writers have declared that the Badmintons are not on the Cotswolds at all! But something has influenced the architecture and I recognize a Cotswold stone and tile when I see one—and here they are a-plenty. However, I would feel strangely alien and servile if I lived in these lovely houses. It doesn't look the place where one would call out to a neighbour, or allow common marigolds to wander outside the neat walls, or kick a conker along the path. And how could one ask for scrag-end at a butcher's shop which sports hanging flower baskets? The Horse Trials office, a low expanse of stone and good tiling, completes a dignified scene.

Provincial tokens issued at Badminton in the eighteenth century are perhaps one of the most interesting insights on the rule of the gentry over the economy. One bronze token shows a beggar asking alms with "I was hungry and ye gave me meat" on the obverse while the reverse is engraved "to the illustrious Duke of

Beaufort, the friend of mankind, and his worthy tenants who reduced the price of their wheat to 9s per bushel. A.D. 1796".

Others are in much the same vein: a wheatsheaf and "relief
against monopoly"; a pair of scales and "3½ lb of bread for 1st
April 1796 God be praised"; a plough and harrows and "success
to the cultivation of waste lands".

What a hoard for the student of economic history.

A more recent and local memory of economics in history was
of Queen Mary who while staying on the Badminton estate during
the war would help cut up logs with a crosscut saw to aid the war
effort.

I forget why I knocked at the door of the thatched cottage on
the corner, perhaps it was to prove that it was real. So gloriously
lop-sided were its windows, so mysteriously darkened were they
from the overhanging thatch that I could not tell if anyone was at
home. After I had knocked I wished I hadn't for such a place would
surely be inhabited by those oh-so-wealthy folks who buy up the
like as a status symbol, leaving it empty half the year while they
migrate to sunnier climes and contributing nothing to village life.
As it happened, no-one was in, but as I stood there thinking such
dark thoughts in the shadows of the heavy thatch I was rewarded
by the countryman's silent answer: onions and honesty hung
golden and silver against the walls.

The fast and furious to-ing and fro-ing of a shuttlecock of
badminton (with a small b) seems hardly compatible with the
elegant hall of Badminton from where it is said to have evolved.
The parish church, attached to the mansion, accommodates the
departed Beauforts, who recline and stand in marble magnificence,
but bear little resemblance to the warm-hearted Beauforts who
may be seen at the horse trials or at their hunts.

Badminton Park, a different concept from that of the early
parco de Badminton, is another punctuation in the passage of
time clothing Cotswold. Acknowledged to be the most sumptuous
grounds in Gloucestershire, the avenues and rides radiating out in
all directions from the mansion reshaped that part of the country,
and it was among the first of the mansions and parks to spread
aristocratic assertion from the seventeenth and eighteenth centuries. It must have been in the mammoth redesigning that the
village of Grumbalds Ash disappeared to make way for the Beau-

fort hunt. Its ghost lingers on in odd names of points on the cross-country course.

Phlox and marigolds, mignonette and thrift and notices saying eggs are for sale edge the older lodge-type cottages that linger outside the great Park wall like hopeful poor relations.

Little Badminton huddles round the village green like a group of happy tousled children round a kitchen table. Thatch, like a heavy fringe, shadows the eyes of the older cottages and the local 'slatters' tidy up the smooth hairline of the Cotswold-tiled pates of the others. The barns seem to have kept the tidiest, as though in close kin to the little church, and bless my soul one might easily mistake one for the other, for no slender spire or lofty tower asserts the latter's superiority of age or authority over the former.

And yet 'tis this homely pile of Cotswold stone, its roofs (for there are two distinct pitches) raised no closer to the heavens nor clad with any greater skill or stuff than those that top the buildings of the farms, that was once the private chapel of the early dukes. Impoverished of ornament it may be, the hand of the Black Death plucking the masons and glaziers from its gilding, but how charming in its simplicity it remains. Prestige without pomp is Little Badminton's greatness.

Across the stony brash that rises from the plough is Petty France, once an eighteenth-century inn, claiming literary reference in Jane Austen's *Mansfield Park*. It was at Petty France that a meeting was held in September 1837 to form a Club "of those Gentlemen who wear the Button of the Duke of Beaufort's Hunt".

Cotswold's Dunkirk—a farm and cottages—edge the A46, the cornfields in late summer as golden as sun-lit sand, with a splash of red poppy reminding us lest we forget another Dunkirk. This spot does not, however, take its name from the tragic Normandy beaches as it is listed as Dunkirk on Isaac Taylor's map of 1777.

A letter in the Records Office, dated 1840, from the G.P.O. reads "the Postmaster of Dunkirk is not required by this Department to use a horse for the distribution of letters in his neighbourhood nor is he paid for the use of a horse in such service by the Postmaster General. If, therefore, he employs one, it is at his own discretion, and does not give him any right of exemption from Turnpike Tolls." Obviously the advent of a new artery of communication was not going to advance at the expense of the other.

It is just coincidence that at this point we should reunite with those who waited for us at Hawkesbury for the ancient trackway calls to us to journey on past Starveall.

Tumuli again rise from the high ground along the route which corresponds so neatly with the main Bath to Stroud road.

Villages did not spring up so readily along the old ridge routes, they owe their existence more to the farming Saxons so we have to deviate somewhat from today's fast-moving traffic, but that is pleasant for one needs to reduce the tempo when surveying villages, for they are nothing to the hasty other than an inconvenient twist of cottage and barn, wobbling cyclists or slow-moving shaggy loads which fill the narrow lanes.

Didmarton on the east has a holy well, which is seldom dry, an ancient church deserted by the Victorian restorers who chose to erect a new one, a mixture of old and new houses, an old manor house and inns, and wooded slopes all round. The road into the village is edged by trees, their shapes elongated like London mannequins and one knows these are the well-bred models outlining the Badminton Estate.

Once a year the villagers make a pilgrimage to the medieval church across the fields to Oldbury-on-the-Hill. Earlier pilgrims left their crosses on its ancient walls.

Knockdown Inn on the Tetbury road must surely have more secular tales to tell. Ahead lies Westonbirt, the world-famous arboretum. So important did the trees become that the village was moved further to the west in order that Robert Holford's conception of a country mansion and grounds could be realized. Certainly the public appreciate the aboretum, managed by the Forestry Commission. It is tempting to lead on into the 116 acres to marvel at the delights each season brings. Green and gold, red and silver, blossom and leaf—endless permutations of life and light, depth and density, shapes and symmetry that make one realize what a meagre diet of adjectives a writer feeds on when faced with such an arboraceous feast. Silk Wood must not be missed out before you explore the delights of 'The Hare and Hounds'; a pint at the bar and snatches of local gossip about Westonbirt's Who's Who or a splendid meal and see Who's Who.

Beverstone House and cottage were designed by Peter Falconer and David Verey—the latter's eminent authority on architecture is nationally acclaimed, this instance of his feeling for traditional Cotswold style locally appreciated.

The castle stands in ruins and long memories, it has had a long tempestuous life. Sheltering Harold while his army quelled the Confessor in 1051, wrapping its stout walls round Stephen when his cousin besieged it in an effort to claim her father's crown, it fell to the Roundheads through the love affair between the young chatelaine of Beverstone and one of Cromwell's officers.

The bones of Cotswold were clothed in the Middle Ages with green once more as arable land reverted to pasture for the vast sheep rearing projects. Beverstone manor lands were stocked with nearly two thousand wethers as soon as Thomas Lord Berkeley bought it and what scenes there must have been—

> To festive mirth, and wit
>   that knows no gall.
> Meantime their joyous task
>   goes on apace
> Some, mingling stir the
>   melted tar, and some,
> Deep on the new-shorn
>   vagrant's heaving side
> To stamp the master's
>   cypher ready stand. . . .

Thomson, like the poets before him brought to life the shepherd's calendar, but it is to the Elizabethans that we turn for a glimpse of the great sheep-shearers' feasting where Perdita "most goddess-like prank'd up" did rule the sway. And that was not a poet's fancy, for Shakespeare was a countryman, and knew Cotswold well. It is interesting to discover the names of both Shakespeare and Hathaway in the old registers of Beverstone.

Chavenage has called the ages together in enigmatic seclusion and Princess Marie Louise gives an interesting vignette of it in her autobiography proving that legends are not simply the stuff of a peasant's fancy. Sleeping in the Cholmondley room, which had been occupied by a renegade Royalist, Princess Marie was aware that some unseen person opened and closed her door; mentioning it to her host she was told that other occupants had experienced the same presence and must have been somewhat relieved by that as she was a distant descendant of the King against whom the turncoat turned. On another occasion her maid saw the Grey Lady who it was thought may have been the sister of Nathaniel Stephens who had pleaded with him to have no part in voting for the execution of the King, predicting a sudden end should he become a regicide.

The sister's presage went unheeded. Retribution followed swiftly. Charles I was executed in January 1649 and Nathaniel Stephens fell mysteriously sick and died in May of that year. Nor was death requital. As the funeral cortege assembled in the great courtyard a splendid coach drawn by fine black horses drew up to the front door driven by a headless coachman arrayed in royal robes on which the star and badge of the Order of the Garter shone magnificently. The coach moved silently away and as it reached the outer gate vanished in flames of fire.

While reflecting on the past, we'll wait awhile again for our other travellers who came by way of the A46. Leighterton, just to the east, is a knot of stone barns, cottages and church caught in a tangled skein of lanes. A stillness lurked in the emptiness of derelict cottages beyond the old church, green scum floated on top of the duck pond, and the early autumn leaves cracked like splintering wood under my feet. Nasturtiums splashed the stone porch and sill with scarlet and gold, their pungent smell filling the small church. Leighterton invites no tourist to record it on celluloid.

It would stretch the ingenuity of any toponymist to convey the almost alpine charm of Boxwell in one word—but what's in a name, anyway? It is a place full of box trees and has a well. The boxwood was extensive in Leland's time and the well, dedicated to St Mary, was accorded with the magical properties of holy wells. Old people remember older people bathing their weak or inflamed eyes in the waters which were believed to be of great curative value.

Lasborough Park, close by, was created in the eighteenth century, the manor much earlier and the church earlier still, but zealous restorers left their mark on it. The village looks lonely enough, but the call of recent wars drew some of its few menfolk from it.

Again a third diversion may have called our companions from the straight road to wander at will along the wooded edges of the hills. But would not our early Cotsaller have been so called? I think he would. Authorities have drawn the Great Cotswold Ridgeway away from the outer edge, but we must remember that they refer to the early trading routes when communication had to be by word of mouth so the old traveller had to save his breath and energy by seeking out the most direct way across the wolds. That is why he cut across to Avening and Sapperton and the high ridge above the Duntisbournes before making for the edge of the scarp again at Birdlip. We will follow in his footsteps again at that point for our communication with the north-west no longer dictates our speed or route, and we have yet to seek out the villages at the westerly edge of the hills.

It is the ancients who left traces of the first real vestige of Cotswold villages. Neolithic man hunted bears, foxes and wolves, bred sheep, goats and pigs, grew wheat and lies in long barrows.

The Celts came next, living much the same life as their Iberian predecessors but, having learnt the use of metals, founded trading routes on which commerce started its long journey through history. They used the horse, ox, sheep, pig and fowl and built round barrows in which to bury their dead.

Buildings and redistribution of trees now shield the tumuli one from the other, and time has covered them with a mantle of turf. How conspicuous they must have been rising from the promontories four thousand years ago, carefully sited so that each could be seen from the next ridge.

These villages of the dead, as I tend to think of them, were not hastily thrown-together efforts. There is a permanence in their construction that man has failed to sustain since. This is our venerable old ancestor, whose name exists nowhere, who first discovered and utilized the stone beneath his feet, which has since distinguished Cotswold building from any other region. Dry stone walls, freestanding and unmortared, were fashioned by him in exactly the same way as they are made today.

My Pop had this inherent skill with stone, many a concaving wall out on the wolds has been straightened by him unknown to the farmer. Picnic spots were always beside a sagging wall. On his 'little look around' Pop would juggle around with the stones, never putting one down—each one has its right place—until "it was put a bit *asum-jasum*". Then, and only then, with a straightened wall at his back, to provide "a bit of burra", and stone dust on his hands would he sit down to his meal. From him I learnt simple complexities of stone. His hands wore a million cracks where the sharp fragments of oyster shells had cut them. A single stone and the landscape of which it is an integral part were as a volume of Cotswold history which he would read. His philosophy seemed to spring also from the earth itself, like many of his ilk he would only accept as fact that which had been proved; substantial, realistic truths that were yet tied to inexplicable laws older than nature itself.

One simple fact that asserts itself, and has been verified by writers much older and more learned than I am, is that Cotswold villages owe their existence to geological factors. It is perhaps poetically pleasing to say they have been born of the earth itself. But it is true. Their bones were formed in the womb of the great Oolite before man was created in flesh and blood. But it took man with his frailties of frame and limb and life to bring forth nature's offspring, to give it light and life and by so doing enriched his own. And from that very fact alone, the Cotsaller's ability to work with nature, springs the secret of why true Cotswold architecture is in complete harmony with the landscape from which it was born. Cotswold philosophy, speech and humour have developed likewise.

Geology is governed by even more ancient and intricate laws so the chapters we read from the Cotswold escarpment has somewhat ragged edges and from Starveall, that familiar name which the Saxons dubbed on every poor bit of land which didn't yield to their plough, the frayed edges are a delight to explore. Sheltered from the screaming east winds by high banks, and teeming motorists by winding lanes, the hamlets seem touched only by the golden fingers of a western sun.

The Kilcotts, Upper and Lower, and Hillesley appeal to the walker but not the motorist: they are reached by steep roads that stretch the calf muscles and fill the lungs with good fresh air to stimulate the appetite for the visual feast of sweeping slopes, dark hollows and knots of trees. Here the springs tinkle in harmony with the sighing grasses, a cow rasps the sweet grass from the earth and man reflects a little on his own inadequacy, for nothing has a more humiliating effect than that of simple rural peace.

On the skyline near Tresham a red harvester crept across a field. Like a huge till it greedily gathered up the dusty gold. I was too far away to hear its drone; too far away for the dry, musty smell to tickle my nostrils or to see the field mice scurry to safer stalks and the white flash of a startled rabbit. But I knew that there within the forest of slippery stems the great metropolis of tiny creatures throbbed with life: a secret world where grasshoppers hopped and worms wiggled and ladybirds gobbled up aphids galore.

Back on top of the road such minute worlds dissolve into perspective, splashes of grey and green and pink and brown again. We can look across wider horizons from our superiority of altitude, for the main road is some 800 feet up, and choose which track we follow. Cloud shadows linger awhile, veiling woods with deep mystery then changing the hues of the wide expanses like a child shuffling coloured shapes. Here and there a spark is fired off a window from a cluster of cottages sheltering into a fold of hill. Great sheets of land have been stitched into neat furrows and a late crop of barley turns its whiskery face back towards the earth as though reminding the impatient harvesters that this is Cotswold country, and 'tis the thin limestone soil that makes the simile 'as slow a-coming as Cotswold barley' no mere figure of speech.

Old and new cottages fold into the hamlets, hollyhocks splash the walls with colour and an old tree, charred and disfigured, crooks like a witch's finger to warn us that not only the friendly elements seek out these spots; and a post office tower reminds us that time has not stood still.

A public footpath is signposted across to Ozleworth, a place of twisting paths, and simple enchantment. Gnarled trunks and rippling streams, tufty grass and tangled brambles seem to have been lifted from Bewick's engravings.

Ozleworth Bottom, as enticing as its name, is one of the most delightful of Cotswold's frayed edges—like an oft-read book it is a place to which one returns to read again of nature's ways. Green upon green stretches forth in spring when rooks startle the silence; a myriad of winged insects dance a Chopin waltz over sun-lit water, ecstatic, ephemeral, in high summer, and when the year closes leaves whisper in their golden age then lie silent as frost and snow outline the beauty of the naked trees.

No one should miss Ozleworth. Antiquarians know of it and the curious will seek it. The motorist will probably come to it by way of Newington Bagpath and be glad that the highwaymen now haunt other realms, for the records will tell you, if the locals forget to, that within the churchyard lies buried the last Englishman to be hanged for highway robbery. Bees often swarm in the church and rabbits burrow beneath it, perhaps making use of the old underground passage that tunnelled towards Lasborough.

Village life is an alliance of man with nature, and here one feels a respect for all powers elemental—be it only that of gravity as the road winds on a high shelf above the Little Avon. The old masons exercised their understanding of these things and their little church stands as proof today. Industry was built on less solid foundations and we find that the Newington weavers died out long before the highwaymen.

The pages of Cotswold's history are stained with decay at Ozleworth Bottom. Ruins of old mills stand beside little streams, giving an impression of timelessness and tranquility which was denied them during their lifetime. Here, perhaps more so than anywhere, geology laid the foundations to be cultivated then exploited by the seventeenth- and eighteenth-century clothiers. It is difficult to reconstruct the scene—for surely that trickle of water never powered the fifteen mills that records say were worked in the five-mile stretch along to Michaelwood. But that was almost two centuries ago. Since then, the springs which came from the hills to feed the streams to power the mills have been tapped near their source by the Water Boards who control the supply to feed the homes and modern industry which has moved to the towns of Dursley and Stroud. It's all rather like "there was an old woman who swallowed a fly", one just hopes that the remedies to alleviate the internal disorders of industry's digestive system take into account the delicate balance of Mother Earth's own constitution.

Tyley Bottom, a smaller twin valley, attracts the rambler with its secret winding paths, little stream and honeycomb of tracks which lead to the Bagpaths. Such devious routes are not for the motorist who will probably remember that he has yet to see Ozleworth church, for he has surely read of its rare hexagonal tower. This has long been a spot for Christian worship as the circular churchyard well illustrates. It is a long avenue that leads to the lonely shrine: the imaginative will flip back the centuries to see again the shadows which could have made a Norman-blooded watchman press closer to the small windows in the many-sided tower. And what, one wonders, was the village like that once stood on the other side of the church?

The religious revolution of the sixteenth century rebuilt in stone as well as faith. With the marks of the battering ram still on them the stones and timbers from nearby Kingswood Abbey were raised into a new work (the stately Newark in its lovely park) for Sir Nicholas Pointz. Of the class to benefit most from the dissolution of the monastic polity, the gentleman must have been eyed with terror by the villagers as his men tore down their churchyard crosses to supplement the stone needed for the grand new edifice, now owned by the National Trust.

Kingswood, maybe because it has become Gloucestershire by legal adoption, does not conform to the county's traditional building style or material. Neither does it seem to wish to comply with that we call a village.

The gatehouse of the ancient abbey serves as a village hall to this little manufacturing centre, and must be one of the most ancient council chambers in the land.

The great clearing operations carried out by the Anglo-Saxon farmers did not denude the entire western edge of its dense woodlands so we see it much about the same as it has been for centuries. The evening sun still glints through the tall trees in tantalizing golden shafts, the bane of motorists making their way down to the old town of Wotton, which was totally destroyed by fire in the reign of King John, and having regained its status as a borough in the thirteenth century it escapes our itinerary.

'Ame', the county's (and possibly the country's) only 'roadwoman' surprised the motorists on their way to Coombe ("Cum" as Ame calls it) for a female roadworker is no common sight. That she found satisfaction in this work comes to us from the record 'Cotswold Characters' which Peter Duddridge and Peter Turner so skilfully recorded with other stories of Cotswold life for the benefit of local hospitals and old peoples' clubs and homes. It is an excellent record and an important collection of social history told by Cotsallers in the rich vernacular Shakespeare knew.

After Ame's candid exposition on the litter-bugs who throw their "pyappers" about for others to "swip up" she endeared herself to me for her vehement declaration to "kip the Cotsall speech a-gwain", illustrating her intention by explaining, "I can speak proper if I wants: I can say 'Good afternoon and how are you'— and I can also say 'Gud aternun an' 'ow bist thee'."

Perhaps the "swit-pyappers" got too much for Miss Cook for

she now travels the roads she used to sweep and grit and shovel as one of "Utton's pwostoomans".

It gets progressively more difficult to see where Dursley ends and Cam begins. Again, like the valley of the Little Avon which burrows into the Cotswolds at Ozleworth Bottom, the one of the Cam, with its abundance of springs, and strata of fuller's earth between the Great and Inferior Oolite, had its natural advantages developed for the clothing industry.

Smyth, the great historian of the Berkeleys, recorded fifty per cent of the population as weavers. Atkyns, looking at the county as a whole a hundred years later, said: "the clothing trade is so eminent in this county, that no other manufacture deserves a mention."

There were about 150 mills and workshops in the Stroud area in its heyday. There are now only four which manufacture in any quantity and they in fact, produce more than all the old mills put together.

Hunt and Winterbotham still have their mill at Cam and employ about 120 people. They told me that the trend is back towards woollen cloth so perhaps synthetic fibres have their days numbered now. The firm has donated its old fulling stocks, which had been in use since the mill was built in 1815 until the mid-1930s, to Stroud Museum. Fulling has only just finished at Cam but the installation of sophisticated machinery means the old woollen industry has a chance of a successful revival in the West Country.

In the old church, rebuilt by Lord Berkeley (an expiatory act, they say, after Edward II's murder at his castle) there lies buried at least one follower of a different calling. A ploughman in seventeenth-century dress is shown in high relief on a table tomb. Farmer Perrott received the sad judgment of being killed by his plough chain for ploughing on a Sunday. I'd wager 'twas a clothier who broadcast that story of divine retribution, but Hodge has a tale to tell of the wicked merchant who stole a statue of St George from the church porch and carried it in his wagon to set up at Colebrook as an inn-sign. The Fates couldn't have deemed that a sin though, for the records are reticent so I suppose the old maxim "God helps him as helps himself but God help him as gets caught" carries some weight!

Cam builders have had no time to delve into the earth for its building stone since the nineteenth century: red bricks, cement-faced breeze blocks and pre-fabs abound, while Spouthouse Lane and Chapel Street remind us how closely knit the distressed and the dissenters were.

But Cam also has long outgrown its village image, like a poor relative 'who's got on a bit in the world' it associates itself with Dursley and shares in that town's increasing industry and prosperity, but here and there old mills crop up like a snatch of gossip from the past.

Old and oft-told tales outlast appearances. Cam Long Down teases the imagination as it lies like a shipwrecked hulk in the Vale beyond. Any feature of the landscape not easily explained was readily ascribed to the workings of the devil, so why bother with geology—anyway, I like this tale much better.

Gloucestershire, of course, is no place for Old Nick—the bell, book and candle were rung, read and lighted back long ago. "As sure as God's in Gloucestershire," we say—a maxim illustrating the extraordinary number of religious houses in the county. Because of this high ratio of church to acreage the devil held a grudge against us. Having devised a scheme by which he would dam the Severn and so flood the people of Gloucester he filled a wheelbarrow with Cotswold stone from the quarry above Dursley and sat down to rest, it being a hot day, quarrying hard work, and anticipation to be savoured. A cobbler came upon the scene, travel-stained and loaded with worn shoes which were strung together around his neck.

"How far to the Severn?" asked the devil.

The cobbler suspecting a 'furriner' showed great cunning: "See these shoes, yellocks," said he, pointing to the many pairs he carried. "I've worn them all out on my journey from the river."

The devil, deterred, tipped his load down into the vale below and so was formed the Long Down.

"Gloucestershire miles be long 'uns," we say, and memories, too! But we shall see where Old Nick played around with the Cotswold stone a little farther along the edge.

With such delicious thrills in folk-lore tales we delight in the knowledge that old customs raise their hoary heads even in this age of science and scepticism.

Thanks to the initiative of Andrew Kennett, a local 'Camian' teacher, the village is richly rewarded with that peculiar cohesion strengthened by tradition which binds people to places. For the past three years he has led the schoolchildren of Cam into the surrounding woods on May Day to gather greenery with which to decorate the school in the same way as their forefathers gathered it to bedeck their homes. Then they wake up the beech trees by knocking on the trunks to remind them it is spring. A May Queen presides majestically and there is Morris dancing. It would be difficult to say that here is the only place to beat the bounds, but there are very few places observing the custom today. And how the children plead to be the one bumped on the chalk mark as they follow the vicar around the boundary.

From the summit of the famous Stinchcombe hill the Severn is a shimmering ribbon threading romance through the flat vale-lands below, Berkeley power station looms up in the distance, pure of line and stark, and the Forest of Dean lies beyond, rugged and dark.

Elder and cow parsley edged the door of Stinchcombe school. I waited awhile hoping to catch at least a glimpse of the dunlin from whose frequentation of this valley the name is derived. But a solitary sparrow fussing at the edge of the drinking fountain housed in a Cotswold stone shelter as a memorial to George Phipps Prevost was the only birdlife I saw. Since those early days when a small sandpiper was a stint the Cotsaller's telescoping of syllables has changed the whole sound of the name.

Names of much more recent import are those of Isaac Williams who lived at one time in the Old Vicarage, and Evelyn Waugh whose home was for a time at Piers Court. An older house behind it claims some association with Prince Rupert.

The tapering tower of North Nibley draws one away, the dull throb of the motorway on the right assuaged by the anodyne of romance for on our left lies Stancombe Park with its hidden lake and secret twisting paths along which, the story goes, the man of the house would meet his lover. Inaccessible from the house and its owner—the gentleman's legal wife no less—the clandestine meetings took place.

The ghostly grottos and shady trees did not afford the couple the complete anonymity they sought, for their names have been scattered abroad: the lass was a gipsy and her lover the vicar of nearby Nibley.

Well, if your Grundyism deters you from visiting the place in

(*above left*) Broadway Tower overlooks thirteen counties; (*right*) Icomb Tower built across a county boundary; (*below*) View from top of memorial tower at Hawkesbury Upton

(*left*) Deserted church tower at Gretton; (*below*) Cooper's Hill, scene of the annual cheese-rolling

Cotswold rick staddles put to new uses (*above*) as an effective 'damp course' for Stanway's thatched cricket pavilion, and (*below*) as a decorative feature to top a wall at Hinchwick

(*above*) Peter Campion, repairing an antique chair; (*below*) Peter Hill, horologist

which the romantic rector preached, your inquisitiveness will better it, for who could resist that honey-coloured building with its low medieval tower. From the churchyard on a plateau the views are extensive. Westbridge Woods hide their bluebells and the Iron Age hill-fort of Brackenbury Ditches.

Grace Smyth kneels in stone, a patient figure who no doubt learnt that virtue during her marriage to John, for his prolific compilations of the Berkeley histories could have left little time for pleasant chit-chat with his spouse.

The village has several interesting old houses but I was struck with the more homely shape of a barn at Southend where harvests have been brought home by the anonyms of the land, and Millmans Farm where John Smyth's clerk is said to have lived. I spared a thought for the poor old scribe whose fingers must have ached with his master's half a century of surveying to the Lords Berkeley.

Nibley Green, quiet enough now, was witness to the skirmish in which Viscount Lisle had his audacity struck down with his life while endeavouring to claim Berkeley Castle. The memorial on Nibley Knoll commemorates a quite different victory. From the main road a green handing-post points the way to Tyndale's monument.

"It's just up there," announced I with enthusiasm. And surely it did look remarkably close as the crow flies, but being more earthbound than he it was a long strenuous upward climb as we went two steps forward and one back on account of the slippery mud track full of loose stones and tangled roots.

There must surely have been a sign at one time to direct weary pilgrims. Up the bank, over a stile, a precipitous climb up the face of the quarry from where the stone for the monument was dug, across a field where vetch and harebells, coltsfoot and clover and scabious nodded only inches from the ground, as though afraid to assert any pretensions to normal height in the shadows of the great tower, under barbed wire and we were there at the foot of the monument. And it was locked!

We ignored the graffiti—although marvelling a little at the pains some people go to in order to add their own insignificant initials and remarks to those of other insignificant people—and recited the well-known fact that William Tyndale "first caused the New Testament to be printed in the mother tongue of his countrymen, born near this spot. . . ."

C

Ray reflected on what the deuce Mrs Tyndale was doing on top of Nibley Knoll at such a time—Alice calculated the economics involved in raising such a monument to mark the occasion and Nen, rubbing a strained calf muscle, wondered what it was that drew such as we to look at it anyway.

As we stood a moment regaining our breath and propriety the setting sun splashed the sky with red and purple, blue and silver and the great loop of the Severn melted into liquid gold. Wales became an inky smudge against the skyline and a thin string of red lights was pulled along the great bridge over the Severn.

Perhaps the ploughboy whom Tyndale declared should be able to read the great book in his own tongue never quite understood all of it, but I felt that this was something he would understand. The countryman's living so close to nature breeds a kind of religion. Paganism? I don't think so. It is a comprehension of seed-time and harvest, of the mightiness and smallness of all things, life and death, daybreak and sunset.

The tower seemed suddenly to lose its substance, the light muted to a soft glow and we remembered what a long way down we had to go, for, as Pop would say "we were up a fair depth". Slithering and sliding to beat the hastening dusk we arrived, mud-spattered and breathless at the bottom, opposite a cemetery. Sustenance can be found in the 'Black Horse'—and the key—and the assurance that there are one hundred and forty-one steps to the top of the tower—and that there is a much easier way up "for them as knows".

Waterley Bottom seemed at first to be a continuation of the mud and trees and secret winding ways. There is no nucleus to the hamlet and one wonders why this spooky spot is inhabited at all. From this secret tract the Waterley Bottom mummers, one of only two bands still in existence in Gloucestershire, take their name to spring to life each Christmas and enact the ancient rites of good fighting evil.

I sought out Owlpen initially for its ghost. And just as elusive it proved to be. The whole of the Stroud valleys were enveloped in dank grey fog, tumps and trunks rose up from nowhere, ancient, hoary, and suddenly. Beech leaves dropped silently, with neither an eddy nor sigh, then the most terrifying storm lashed out. Tree trunks buckled through the shivering rain and a ragged black outline between spiky firs brought a screech from me and the car brakes.

Private property? we contemplated as an old door barred an entrance between stone pillars into the woodland.

"Doesn't say so," said I with the simple philosophy that if you're not told you don't know.

With great temerity we made our way through the next, un-gated, entrance. Winding through young firs we were suddenly faced with a grand gatehouse, but it was the broken outline of a deserted ruin back in the trees that caught my attention and sent shivers down my spine. Dusk gathered swiftly around its ragged shape and an owl hooted somewhere from amid the dense woodland. A shaft of yellow light snapped across our path and we turned in its direction. Faces pressed against a downstairs window in the gatehouse, and we agreed that it was only right and proper that we should explain our being on what may be private property which I assured Ray was a man's job—well, it was teeming with rain! A few minutes later he returned, dripping wet. The couple vowed there was no village, church or ghost. The square of light was suddenly shut off as the lady of the household hastily drew the curtains, her face crinkled through the thousand rivulets on the window pane—she looked bewildered and we certainly felt it.

There is no such conjecture about Uley. The neolithic path-finders found it as they made their way about close to the highest ground. We can still have our fill of the fine views across the Severn valley, softly rounded hills and the dark mass of the Forest of Dean as Stone Age man had. And when he had witnessed the last sunset drawing earth and sky together he went to rest in the Cotswold hill in chambers lined with Cotswold stone, to be sought out by the Roman invader whose curiosity was probably as keen as our own to learn a little of the kin of the Stonehenge builders. Here is an outstanding example of the neolithic long barrows which punctuate our hills.

Uley itself is said to be from 'yew-tree glade or clearing', but as very few stone axes have been found on the Cotswolds it would seem that there was very little woodland to clear.

The seventeenth century brought a new name to the most impressive of the fifty or so long barrows, Hetty Peglar's Tump, after an Edith Peglar whose family owned the land on which it stands.

The need of water-power for the fulling mills brought great industry to the village below the prehistoric camp and the fame of Uley blue cloth was equalled only by that of Stroud scarlet.

The industry was not as spiritually satisfying as *Observations on the Necessity of Introducing Machinery into the Woollen Manufactory* would have us believe when "on a fine summer day to view the aged matron carding wool before the door of the rural cottage, the young children handing the fleecy rolls to their parents, while the cheerful song of the healthy village damsels uniting with the whirring spindle complete the rural harmony. . . ."

A different picture emerges from the evidence of Erasmus Charlton, a police officer whose duties included searching houses for stolen yarn. He saw no poetry in poverty.

"The weavers are much distressed, wretchedly off for bedding, a man his wife and seven children sleep on straw on the floor covered over with a torn quilt. The children cry for food, the parents have neither food nor money in the house or work to obtain any. . . ."

A good meal seemed to be limited to a few potatoes with flick (fat from the inside of a pig) melted and poured over them. ". . . I do not think that one family out of ten can go to church because of ragged conditions."

Church attendance declined not so much through the congregation's awareness of its poor apparel as its awareness of a totally different persuasion which was gaining a foothold in the distressed areas. United in a common plight and religion the dissenters enjoyed a certain cohesion housed at Uley in a Union Chapel designed to hold almost five hundred people—the first in that neighbourhood.

The long village nurses many memories in its small cottages, forgotten streams, old inns, and elegant eighteenth-century houses built with the wealth from trade. Only an outsize doorway or arched entrance speak of a former role. Students of economic history know so well the climactic steps which culminated in the riots. The stirring times are mere words today in the County archives which tell of employers being dragged to the duck ponds, lives and property being saved only by the intervention of a troop from the Tenth Hussars.

The developing iron works drew many of the work-starved workers into South Wales, the new railroads took others to lay tracks across the breadth of the country, while others sought salvation in other climes. As I pored over the accounts of expenses in a quiet corner of the Records office I wondered what the thoughts of those emigrants were as they embarked for the new countries.

Fed *en route*, conveyed free, and regaled in clothing to the value of £1 10s 8¾d each, which sum included a prayer book and bible, at the expense of parish or government rates, scores of Cotsallers ebbed out of Bristol on whose water the early Dobuni had drifted in.

But what of those too sick or too old to make a new life? The Minute Books of the Workhouse draw an incredibly pathetic picture of the paupers' existence in which 'Crust Water' seemed to be a regular suppertime drink. Relief came to others in the shape of a Parish coffin. An appalling side of the Poor Law is brought to light in an investigation of 1839 when a Mr Holloway was criticized for making thin coffins for the Poor of Uley and on one occasion declared "I do not consider it part of my business to screw the top on for the 9 shillings." O, callous Avarice.

I took to the hills behind the village and wandered aimlessly into a tiny tower, deserted by the world except for a few birds, and roofed only by overhanging branches, and tried to imagine it in its former days, its rough-hewn walls echoing to the rough-bluff tongue of the Stroud valleys. Watching a spider making its interminable journeying round and round, and up and down, its slender thread catching up crossing paths, the whole being a thing of incredible beauty and ingenious skill and planning—which I could have destroyed with one flick of a finger—a paragraph from Palmieri's *La Vita Civile* snapped across my thoughts. On natural philosophy he agreed that the "investigations of the secrets of nature were in themselves not unworthy of study but are of the minutest interest in the supreme task of solving the problem how to live."

Then I remembered the many references in the old records to the apathy of the weavers when neighbouring farmers offered them work. Having farming Saxon blood in my veins I understood not the ways of the weavers so made off for Frocester to sniff again the musty dusty straw in one of England's finest barns.

Pedants will cry, "Frocester—Cotswold?" And I will reply, from whence hailed those stones of yon walls, and the slats which roof those walls, and the corn and fleece which were stored within those walls—from Cotswold my friend.

What vast estates the Benedictine monastery must have covered to have filled this superb collecting house with tithes; perhaps the old Abbot de Gamage was not so good at his fractions—for thousands of tenths would have warranted such an edifice. Whatever his accounting system for collecting the tithes may have been the net result is still today an enrichment of the landscape. A ladder on top of the sea of stone slates was an assurance that the owner was going to make sure that it stayed that way.

The main road into Stroud runs along the edge from which the expanse of vale beyond may seem flat and dull to the hill-folk or lush and fruitful to the Cobbetts.

The Stanleys, Leonard and King's respectively, sound an interesting couple but they appear not of Cotswold kin, very little stone runs through their veins despite their origins being from a stony clearing (*stān lēah*).

King's is distinguished from Leonard on account of the manor being an ancient demesne of the crown. Pre-fabs, mauve doors, yellow window frames, white walls, puce gates, and blue bressumers run riot through the villages—nay, they do not separate from each other and cohere within their own confines to qualify as villages— as though the children ran from their black-and-white primary school to paint the buildings themselves. But this puerile picture is that of a cursory glance; get out of the car and find in this home of the Mercian royalty and the Roman nobleman the fifteenth-century hall-house, good farmhouses, Stanley House, and the first fire-proofed building in England in the shape of Stanley Mill.

Has cousin Leonard as much to offer? Indeed it has. A prominent earthworks was reckoned to have been a Roman refuge from Irish raiders, and the west window of the church is said to be the first of William Morris's ecclesiastical stained glass work.

An air of mystery links the ancient buildings with the priory of St Leonard. An early Saxon church is used now as a farm-building. Students of architecture study its herringbone masonry and seek out the tithe barn which has a medieval traceried window, while less-informed beings will think the pond is a common duck-pond whereas its origin was that of providing the brethren with their own fresh fish.

Monks seem to be an over-worked faction of the spectral world, their flowing robes adding fluidity to the scene, and the brothers of St Leonard's Priory do their stint, according to the clock-winder of the church who felt the presence of someone beside him. It is not only the more secular maintenance of his former home that the ghostly monk checks on; he has been seen at the celebration of communion.

The organist of Stroud Parish Church cast a different light on the brotherhood in his curious poem of 1824

> At Leonard Stanley there's an ancient church,
> Where Roman Catholics will wont to search
> For miracles and relics that will give
> To any sinful wretch a quick reprieve,
> The artful monks to cheat the humble poor,
> Were hid in winding passages secure
> To mimic supernatural voices when
> They wanted to defraud their fellowmen.
> The priory adjoins where the nuns
> Pored o'er their beads and veiled their faces once,
> Is now a farmer's dwelling richly stor'd
> With all that's needful for the festive board.
> The place where devotees and Friars trod,
> Bearing the host which they revered as God,
> Is now a haunt for poultry, geese and swine,
> Where people feed and milk their useful kine.

Stroud, 'the strewed bit' of Bisley manor, grew up from a hamlet to a town of eminence by the time Henry VI was on the throne. The deep valleys over which we have rambled have drained to the Severn in dramatic descent and despite the relatively small streams that tumbled over the Cotswold edge to enrich the pasture of the vale below, they were harnessed to provide the water power to supply the mills of the west.

Stonehouse would be an appellation suited to almost any Cotswold village, but would not have been so readily used if stone had been a common building material of Norman England. The extensive woodlands made timber the more easily obtained; the arduous task of quarrying was only undertaken for the prominent and eminent buildings. We may be assured in this case that here, then, was some manorial residence built of the stone usually reserved for castles and churches.

Now it is difficult to define Stonehouse as a village proper, so

close to Stroud does it lie, but to it are ascribed the only vine-
yards of Gloucestershire at Domesday. Here, Elizabeth I slept peace-
fully one night, and George Whitefield roused the folks up one
day.

A slender spire rises elegantly between distant trees, and one
can take in the good clean air which makes this such a splendid
choice for the famous hospital as the low hill projects towards
Standish from the Cotswold scarp. Much history is hoarded up
within the little village. It felt the rude hand of civil war and
Robert Frampton, Bishop of Gloucester, received the cold wind of
deposition for refusing to acknowledge Dutch William. An idyllic
picture of country contentments is presented by the Butter Beech,
under whose boughs the milkmaids marketed their dairy produce.
It remains just a memory now, more's the pity.

Tall chimneys rise up from a Cotswold-styled house in front of
Haresfield church which has one of the nine lead fonts in the
county. A tooth, believed to be six hundred years old, and an
epitaph penned by the great Dryden to a little John, are on dis-
play.

Pretty thatch catches the eye and a stone sundial tells us it is
time to return to the hills where last century thousands of coins
minted fifteen hundred years before were found in the old Roman
camp. A stone on another hill commemorates the siege of Gloucester.

Social reformists will be off to Hardwicke to nod approvingly at
the juvenile criminals' reformatory started last century and shake
their heads disapprovingly at its closure. The A419 on which
they travel is based on more material foundations: the two-mile
stretch between Little Haresfield and Hardwicke being built on the
causeway constructed by the monks of Gloucester in the thirteenth
century of sufficient strength and width to bear the wheeled traffic
to cope with the expansion of rural economy of that period. I took
again to the winding lanes which no doubt were sealed to the earth
in the tracks made by the cattle and their followers.

A horseshoe over the doorway of a cottage was a delicious reminder that old beliefs linger long. A little wash-house with a curl
of smoke from its chimney was evidence that the old ways had not
yet died out either.

Maybe the lady of the household would often wish her old fire-
copper away in lieu of a gleaming tin box which would pummel

her linen in suddy secret when the wind made the smoke 'duff down', who knows. But I could picture the scene later in the year when the little timber and thatch cottage might smell of dark fruits and spices and the snowy-capped basins would be plunged into the deep belly of the old copper in its own little brick house in the garden.

Other preparations for the later year were not in my imagination. Ditches were being dug deep alongside the narrow lane in readiness for the winter rains. A black-and-white farm dog had more immediate things to attend to, and I marvelled at the authority he asserted over a herd of Friesians to get them into a field of buttercups, and marvelled again, without admiration, on the reason for the latest threat of scientific warfare—Operation of Extermination of all Buttercups.

A notice warns that it is 'No thru road' down the lane that leads to the small church. Norman earls had a castle hereabouts in this patch of Cotswold where you run ankle-deep in summer buttercups and trudge ankle-deep in winter mud.

Nut bushes, brambles and ferns cling tenaciously to the narrow roadway as it climbs steeply up. The stones in the walls are large and squared and do not conform to the 'one above two' principle of dry-stone walling until the sharp ascent brings one abruptly into Edge. And there are the thin ragstone layered walls again topped with 'cummers' over which you can look at the Vale of Gloucester gleaming in misty sunlight.

The valleys of this westerly edge are well worth seeking out so I make no excuse for hoping the traveller will go up one side and back along the other for no roads actually cross them. So let us double back a bit and even if we have to travel the same road twice all but the impatient will forgive me—I would expect no remission if I had failed to point out that from Haresfield Beacon the most majestic prospects in all England may be viewed.

Clouds scud so low over Scottsquarry Hill that I fear they will surely knock over the solitary figure on top, but all is well and he and his dog perch on the edge of the great ridge of the steep hill looking down at me looking up. And I can see what is holding them up—wide seams of creamy-coloured limestone. But it is to the Beacon we must hurry to see what Cotswold is made of for it is a geologist's dream. And what better place from which to view the temperamental 'Sabrina' creating the phenomenal Bore.

A gradient 1 in 4 gouges a road through the tumps. Gloucester on one side and Stroud on the other lie in their own valleys, and on most days it could just as well be the sea on either side, white-edged clouds the rolling breakers. I, of course, in blissful ignorance once thought that I would be able to reflect on the glories of Haresfield over a long drink at the Beacon Hotel—to find it faced a railway crossing, so it was back up the hill, past the lovely old oaks to the Beacon proper whereupon I reflected on the Trades Description Act and wondered whether nomenclatures were excluded.

And what a riot that would be if our ancestors were called to account for the oddities that pepper the Cotswold tithe maps.

"Scottsquarry—to which Scot did it belong?"

"None m'lord, 'tis but Old English scēot for steep."

"Well, why didn't you say so—aah, aah—Bacchus I see—worshippers of the vine, eh?"

"Not so, m'lord, 'tis from that other great staff of life and came from bake-house."

"Mm. Cat's Castle?"

"Well, 'tis not rightly a castle as you'd reckon on now, m'lord —'twas a common enow thing to call a barn a castle."

"And it was always said you prided yourselves on calling a spade a spade—if I may quote a more recent expression."

"When it comes to the land, m'lord, there aint no argufying 'bout she—there's no gadling there. Good lands be Fat pockets and Fillhorn and bad 'uns be Nevergaine, Littleworth, Long Friday, Starveall, Twistgut and Scrat arse."

And if the Cotsall speech raises a superior smile from a parvenu I would challenge him to define it for it confounds analysis. The true exponent speaks it but never writes it—he leaves that to those "long-headed myun as knows nothing about it whatsomever."

I well recall my grandfather chanting these lines to me from A Cotswold Village which he called his Cotsall Bible, having the greatest respect for the gentle erudite Arthur Gibbs who "said sommut every time he spoke."

> If thee true Glostershire wouldst know
> I'll tell thee as to allus zay un
> Put I for me and a for o
> On every possible occasion

When in doubt squeeze in a w
Stwuns for stones; and don't forget zur,
That thee must stand for thou and you
Her for she, and vice versa.

Put v for f, for s put z
Th and t we change to d
Zo dry an kip this in thine yud
An' thou'st wilt talk as plain as we.

2

Harescombe to Lower Quinton

HARESCOMBE TO LOWER QUINTON

As we shall be exploring the delights of the Painswick valleys in a later chapter we should follow along the base of the hills if only for the sheer enjoyment one gets from climbing back on to them again. Brown ponies in small orchards and milk churns edging the road which runs into Brookthorpe are stoic reminders that village life will go on even in such close proximity to a motor-way.

Brookthorpe bred sterling posties. Postman George Herbert was so appreciated by the villagers for his services, which extended to doing odd jobs and delivering Granny Davis's washing to the Vicarage, that they gave him a splendid easy chair on his retirement.

Villagers still talk of old Miss Walter's big bed on which she sat amongst the postage stamps. Being crippled with rheumatism she was unable to move easily so customers helped themselves to the wares displayed on the dresser and took them to the bed to pay for them. Of such stuff are villages made, but for those whose interest is roused more by things national rather than local there is a fascinating chronogram in the church porch:

> *Ter Deno IanI Labens reX soLe Co Dente*
> *CaroLVs eXVtVs soLIo sCeptroqVe seCVre*

The letters which are roman numerals add up to 1648, the fateful year in which Charles I lost his throne and sceptre and head.

We head towards Gloucester, passing over the M5, not as historians following the fate of a deposed king but to look at a chunk of Cotswold which was cast off from the main mass before history began.

The first of the three outliers of Cotswold, Robin's Wood Hill, formerly known as Mattes Knowle from its Norman lords of the manor, now perpetuates the memory of the Robins family who raised sheep on its land for over two centuries. A new feature of the hill had its beginnings as a start of '1973 The Year of the Tree' when one hundred trees were given by the Gloucestershire branch of Men of the Trees towards the countryside park being made on the side of the hill.

When Jubilee Grove and Founder's Grove reach maturity the local children, then also mature, will look back to that chill November day when Dr Richard St Barbe Baker held a slim ash sapling for the Duke of Beaufort to plant the first tree.

They may, perhaps, tell their children of the elderly gentleman who was educated at Cheltenham and came to the Cotswold hill that day and, I hope, be able to point to a patch on the atlas and say, "those two million square miles of agricultural land were once part of the great Sahara desert, but thanks to the foresight of Dr Baker who founded the Men of the Trees Society in 1922 to show people how important trees are to life, the scheme he started has reclaimed all that waste land to produce food again."

At Upton St Leonards I came across another of the small family communities which have settled in the Cotswolds. Geographically the Taena Community is self-contained, but not enclosed or isolated from society. A group of five families live on a farm at Whitley Court which has its own chapel and carry out their skilled crafts in woodcarving, pottery, silver work and sculpture.

I set out for Sneedhams Green with my rustic nose twitching— 'a homestead on the detached piece of land'. The homestead turned out to be blocks of flats: tall, straight boxes, garish patches of colours giving the only touch of individuality. A chained pig on the square green struck an incongruous note, giving an ancient touch to the open common: a reminder that enclosure didn't fully affect Upton St Leonards—in which parish it is—until the turn of the century.

Common grazing rights at Brockworth are preserved by the

Whit Monday cheese-rolling ceremony on Cooper's Hill, or at least that is one version of why this custom takes place. But as the County Records show the cheese-rolling to date back over 1,300 years it speaks of more ancient origin. 'Paganism' is whispered because it was a Midsummer event in those days, an important point in the calendar of early folk. The round cheese could there-fore symbolize the sun. Another theory is that it is an annual cele-bration of victory. Who against whom? History speaks of the Dobuni being harassed by the Silurian people of the west—perhaps the hill was saved from attack by the nomadic Silures being caught off balance by the Dobuni hurling cheeses down on them from the top: Double Gloucesters, no doubt! Not quite as facetious a remark as it first appears—when those cheeses come spinning down a veritable one-in-one gradient the momentum is pheno-menal. It would be a brave—nay! a suicidal—trick to face such an onslaught. The cheeses, said to be 'as hard as Fayrur's [Pharaoh's] heart' seem to suffer little damage, being usually intact when caught.

A programme which survives from last century speaks of the ceremony being quite an elaborate affair and included the following events:

2 cheeses to be ron for (down the hill)
1 plain cake to be green for (the contestants had to grin through 'hoss collards' [horse collars] the best grin gained the prize)
1 plain cake to be jumpt in the bag for
Horings to be dipt in the toob for (oranges and apples were dipped for in a tub of water)
Set of ribbons to be dansed for (these were the ribbons worn by the Master of Ceremonies)
Shimey to be ron for (chemise run for by the girls)
Belt to be rosled for (the men wrestled for the belt worn by the Master of Ceremonies)
A bladder of snuff to be chatred for by hold wimming (It is not clear whether the winner was the old woman who chattered the loudest or the longest)

By 1890 the chattering, grinning and wrestling were replaced by a flower show with tug-of-war and climbing the maypole. The pole is by tradition one grown in Witcombe Wood and was until recently replaced annually, the Commoners fearing they would lose their rights otherwise. In fact the Commoners who have rights tied to their properties still enjoy the ancient privileges.

When I last went to ramble over the hillside an enormous wigwam of brushwood at its base promised a spectacular bonfire night. Perhaps the great cheese doesn't count as an 'object'; the Romans got there before the Parish Council; and the latter's power of vehicular propulsion (or imagination or temerity) must be mightier than most it if considers the driving of cars or riding of motorcycles a necessary prohibition along with those banning the rolling of objects and the setting up of camps on the hill.

Cooper's Hill, however, is there to be enjoyed, being a local nature reserve of about 137 acres owned by Gloucestershire County Council, and is a permanent nature trail. To those who enjoy panoramic views almost all of the Severn Vale can be seen on a good day extending from the Severn Bridge in the south to the Malverns and Bredon Hill in the north, with the Sugar Loaf and the Black Mountains of Wales due west. To those whose interests are aroused by their immediate surroundings they will delight in the large whitebeam overhanging the car park, the beech and ash, the bracken and bramble, the holly and hawthorn, violets and wood sanicle, yellow archangel and fireweed and the feeling of antiquity on the largest of Cotswold's Iron Age camps.

From the top where a maypole perches so perilously close to the edge as to render it superfluous except as a base for the weathercock it supports, the white spirals of smoke from industrial Gloucester suspend like so many interrogation marks over the flat plain out of which another lump of Cotswold raises its head. Churchdown Hill, the second outlier of the ancient escarpment, forms a conspicuous topographical feature in the flatlands between Gloucester and Cheltenham.

The Romans used the earthworks they found on the hill and a sturdy Norman tower makes one think that it is a castle that looks down from the wooded prominence, but it is another of the great Gloucestershire churches. The hill was not, however, named on account of the church: *cruc* and *dun* tell of the 'round hill'.

A television booster aerial raises a slender finger from the summit and extensive reservoirs hold water supplies for the nearby towns. The marlstone rock is not good building material, the frost picks out the large fossils leaving the stone pocked and gnawed; its virtues lie in its ability to retain water to be released by springs lower down the hill. When the lord of Churchdown—Roger, Archbishop of York, planned to supply the village with water from one of the springs his engineer was buried alive when the earth fell in on top of him—some twenty-odd feet below the surface. Invoking the aid of St Thomas, he miraculously survived to be dug out the following day.

The shifting foundation set many a tree on the slopes at a drunken angle and gorse bushes and pine trees give this outlying hill distinctive features. The upper slopes afford a natural habitat for badgers who can dig out the sandy soil easier than the hard limestone or the sticky clay.

Badgeworth, close by, does not owe its etymology to badgers, but has two special claims to fame. It is one of the most ancient parishes in the kingdom and contains the smallest nature reserve in which a rare species of buttercup is to be found.

Jealous guard of bell-casting comes to light by these rhymes inscribed on a bell:

> Badgeworth ringers, they were mad
> Because Rigbie made me bad;
> But Abel Rudhall, you may see
> Hath made no better than Rigbie

Vicious word from iron tongues.

Brockworth itself is so close to Gloucester that I was startled to find a rabbit bobbing along the main road, but why not? This is the ancient Ermine Way and it is said that it was the Romans who introduced the rabbit to our island so run rabbit, run—thy ancestry is as lineal as thy roads are linear.

A right hand turn at the Cross Hands Hotel draws the Roman road up to Birdlip. Notorious for icy patches and fog each in their season, the hill winds up steeply beneath beech trees that elongate to reach the sun. The spirit of the old road haunts it still and I fancy I hear the low curse of a driver, a crack of leather, the sound of iron upon the loose stone road and wonder how many noble beasts had strained their hearts before the special dispensation (signed by Robert Raikes—founder of the *Gloucester Journal* and father of Robert Raikes whose Sunday School became famous) allowed extra horses to share the excruciating task. It is only the wheezing of low-geared engines which now comes to the rambler who chooses to walk across to Barrow Wake.

(*above*) Snowshill alone on the high wolds; (*below*) Ruins of Hailes Abbey

Cotswold stone: (*top*) Peter Juggins with his completed set of pinnacles on Fairford's famous wool church; (*right*) Peter Juggins stone carving; (*bottom*) 'Pop' stone walling

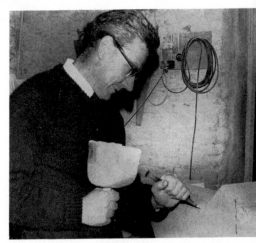

(*above*) A sweep of a Cotswold dry stone wall at Pitham Bottom near Quenington; (*below*) A Cotswold stone quarry

(*above*) The quaintly styled Fish Inn, Broadway; (*below*) Tunnel House at Coates built as an inn for the canal workers

We are again at a point where the ages of man meet. Prehistoric man passed this way on the ancient trading route and a lady of the Dobuni slept by the roadside before the Roman invasion. As I marvelled at the craftsmanship of the bronze mirror found in her grave, now preserved in Gloucester Museum, puzzling as to whether the intricate design picked out in red enamel was of any esoteric significance, I couldn't help wondering what had been reflected in that lovely object. Was the face young and fair, the eyes bright or sad? Whatever her physical features, her spirits must have risen as ours do whenever we pass this way, for here is one of the most spectacular viewpoints of our hills.

Only the very hasty pass along this road at a normal speed. Even the overflowing litter baskets from those who paused to feast on the sheer beauty and prepacked snacks cannot spoil the glory of this spot. The majesty of the escarpment cannot be defiled by paltry crisp-bags.

It is another prominent site on which one has come to expect a monument. It has one, but it is small—*Multum in parvo*—a simple stone indicator on which 500 million years of geology can be read. It is a lovely thing to have here and a fitting memorial to Peter Hopkins whose epitaph reads quite simply: "Geologist and Christian 1932–66."

The tumpy grass has been worn into narrow sandy tracks on the hill's summit. Gloucester shimmers far below and I hid the whole city from view by holding up one hand—such is the power of perspective. The absence of trees in the immediate vicinity gives a wide vista across to Crickley Hill where an Iron Age fort—one of the most important ever found in southern England—has recently been excavated. From what I gather from the Local History Bulletin there are plans afoot to preserve and restore it as far as possible to its original form: a great asset to the Cotswolds if it does materialize.

This is the most dramatic scenery of the Cotswolds—a geologist's mecca. Who would, of course, explain the great pedestal at the extreme edge of the hill as a natural formation caused by erosion, but we know it is the Devil's Table.

The 'Air Balloon' pub stands close to the roundabout and we take the road past Ullenwood Manor where our friends at the National Star Centre for Disabled Youth receive such splendid training in the field of further education.

D

Leckhampton Hill is a place of associations. It was the

> November evenings! Damp and still
> They used to cloak Leckhampton Hill

that tantalized the young James Flecker to write one of his last poems as he lay dying in Switzerland.

To a cyclist the hill is a test of endurance or an exhilarating ride, depending upon his ascending or descending; a hill-land for the people. And like most freedom it had to be fought for—nothing military or a reference hidden in the mists of obscurity.

1902 brought an Owner who raised fences and employed a hunchback keeper to keep the people off His Hill. But he had reckoned without the People. In their hundreds they swarmed up Their Hill, burnt down the fences and the keepers' cottage and a band played merrily the while. The owner lost his fight for sole possession and as Milton said, "None can love freedom heartily but good men" so the victory was celebrated every Good Friday until a bigger threat to our land took precedence. But what strange beings we are. Freedom of a single hill was a victory to be celebrated for almost four decades—that of all Britain, not a murmur!

"Such dupes are men to custom." And even the O.S. acquiesce, for there on the map is *Devil's Chimney* of which Ruff wrote in the *History of Cheltenham* in the early nineteenth century, "built by the devil, as say the vulgar. It was no doubt built by shepherds in the frolic of an idle hour."

So—vulgar we must admit to be! But a bit more *au fait* with the tending of flocks than the historian—"the frolic of an idle hour" forsooth! The rocks chipped out by the shepherds' crooks? And what do our friends the geologists say?

"A quarryman's joke made about 1780." But the column of stone is more likely to have been left "as it was not good enough to be used as building stone."

The Chimney has shown definite signs of erosion lately. The report of its possible disappearance from the Cotswold scene brought forth quite a few letters to the local paper. The stones that came from this hill to build Regency Cheltenham below can be knocked down and reshaped into any design to appease the planners but action is called for to preserve the land-mark Cheltonians have lived with for so long. Old Nick must have mellowed with the limestone in which he settled, or did he vacate this spot long ago, for Yarleys, exploring the Hill with the keen eye of a child, found a huge stone shaped like a bed in a small cave at the end of the quarry. The countryman's equivocal manner of attributing any phenomena to be the works of the deity or the devil, the stone was called Jacob's Bed.

To avoid Cheltenham's town centre a pretty drive is up the A435 to Seven Springs where a little thatched toll house sports posters of local events. The A436 runs eastwards and gorse bushes speak of the ground hereabouts having been disturbed. Archaeologists have discovered traces of cultivations in the area dating back over 3,000 years.

Old Cold Comfort, once a seventeenth-century coaching inn, stands on the slope of Foxcote Hill. It is said that a natural cleft in the ground opposite was over 100 feet deep. It is a place that has attracted ghost stories in its isolation, tramps and the homeless in its desolation and a handsome price in its recent restoration.

Dowdeswell is a small village with a big Court, enormous ivy leaves, a fine square house with eight gables, very steeply pitched stone-tiled roofs, a church bell inscribed "when I was cast into the ground, I lost my tone and revived my sound 1658", an inn named after the reservoir it faces and the usual ornate Waterworks house as the road leads back towards Cheltenham where it is reputed the last shepherd in England to be hanged for sheep-stealing haunts the fields around Black Barn.

The struggle to retain the character of our Cotswold villages has given birth to many conservation and preservation societies, but Prestbury has a particular problem. Lying as it does on the road to Cleeve Hill and Winchcombe one hears it described as "the pretty bit leading out of Cheltenham", although the little iron-railed balconies on which the townsfolk bobbed and waved to the royalty who came to 'take the waters' do not extend round the corner into Prestbury proper.

The suburban tag is aggravated by the fact that when the race meetings moved to their present site they brought the title Cheltenham Races with them. But it is Prestbury soil on which the legendary Arkle and Pat Taaffe mastered the strenuous uphills and tricky downhills of the natural amphitheatre below Cleeve Hill to win three Gold Cups in successive years.

Prestbury's own phenomenal son of the turf "the greatest

wonder that ever crossed a horse" was born in 1857 in a room
above a stable backing on the derelict chapel graveyard—although
a plaque in St George's Place informed disciples otherwise. There
is no such dispute about the place where the great Fred Archer
received his early riding lessons. The 'King's Arms', a lovely old
timbered inn, preserves the shoe of his first mount, and a plaque
informs us that it was here "he swallowed his earliest porridge",
and trained "upon toast and coffee and Cheltenham water".

Racing history began last century when the infamous Colonel
Berkeley gave a thousand pounds to help steeplechasing gain the
popularity which flat racing lost. By the time of Wellington's
third visit the thundering hooves were pounding the Prestbury
turf which was classed "by judicious sportsmen as equal, if not
superior, to any in the kingdom."

> I remember the lowering wintry morn,
> And the mist on the Cotswold hills,
> Where I once heard the blast of the huntsman's horn
> Not far from the Severn rills.
>
> Jack Esdaile was there, and Hugh St Clair,
> Bob Chapman and Andrew Kerr,
> And big George Griffiths on Devil May Care
> And Black Tom Oliver

wrote Adam Lindsay Gordon—since accorded a memorial plaque
in the Poet's Corner of Westminster Abbey.

'Black Tom' Oliver, mentioned in that poem *Legend of Cotteswold*, was a great rider of gipsy stock whose Prestbury stables
turned out Grand National winners—himself being one thrice. Jack
Esdaile, another fine rider was married to Ianthe Shelley, daughter
of the poet who penned the evocative lines in Lechlade churchyard.

History lurks everywhere in Prestbury—Bouncers, Burgage,
Prior's Piece, Lake Street, the Priory—names clamouring for
attention to their past. Ghosts haunt the buildings and streets but
it is not the nocturnal wanderings of a mystic monk, footsteps at
twilight or the strains of a spinet that disturbs Prestburians. The
shivers that run down Prestbury's ancient spine would start with
some development officer's pencil on a drawing board. It is hoped
that the spirit of indiscriminate re-developers will be exorcised
by the powers of the C.P.R.E.

I am delighted to read in the local paper that "Prestbury has resisted the overtures by the borough council to incorporate the parish within the borough on a number of occasions because it prefers to retain its unique identity and village atmosphere." Three cheers for the Parish Council. It is a village of ancient charm, good buildings of stone and timber and thatch, thrills and motley of the National Hunt Festival, well-groomed horses, country tweeds, friendly old pubs and a thatched baker's shop where one can buy good old-fashioned bread straight from Mr Fogarty's ovens.

I will not digress along the picturesque lanes and lovely foot-paths which lead to Cleeve Hill where the air is pure, the views spectacular and the Cotswolds rise to their highest point (1,083 feet). The ancient track took prehistoric man across its open land. The walker and lover of Pennine-like scenery and the golfer will know it. It was here that racing at 'Cheltenham' began as a three-day event in 1819 and six years later was attracting some 40,000 people. It was to Cleeve Hill that some of Britain's top song-writers took their newly acquired racehorse *The Songwriter* to be trained by Col. Jack Gibson.

Other horses and animals have been taken to Cleeve Hill over the last five years for less temporal reasons. Pet lambs, cats, dogs, horses and donkeys are taken each year by their owners to a unique open-air service which Mr and Mrs Peter Deakin organize at their home, Hayme's Farm. A delightful way of including 'all creatures great and small' in divine thanksgiving.

It was from Cleeve Hill that Leland must have meant the "fine stone of Prestburie" was quarried to build "Tewkxburie Abbey". What a strange chess-board religion has laid out on which the noble players shifted stones of abbeys as pawns in their game of power, for the hall in nearby Southam's great house is paved with painted tiles from Hailes across the valley.

Woodmancote and Bishop's Cleeve wear a different style as we skirt the hills to see dwiles being flonked at Gotherington. Before the curious reach for a dictionary, head for the village or report the fact to the Board of Censors let me hasten to add that it does not appear in the former and only on August Monday in the latter, and the vicar knows all about it.

The village wears the garb of Shakespeare's country whose close neighbour it is. Old and new blend together quite pleasantly and even complement each other: thatched Elm Tree cottage, a modern Primary School and monastic-styled windows since built up in The Folly leads one past a lovely old oak close by Pardon Hill Farm and to the foot of diminutive Dixton Hill.

Roads lead off westwards to Teddington where today's speeding motorist casts but a cursory glance in the direction of the many-fingered handing-post—a curiosity in these days of tin-plate signs. Beyond, Bredon Hill, the last and largest of the three Cotswold outliers, rises up from the Evesham Vale. The hill is outstandingly beautiful, being preserved from the scars of metalled roads for none actually cross it. It is true limestone country, laced with dry-stone walls, studded with clumps of beech, and gouged by old quarries. Its numerous springs have resulted in a fine outcrop of village and the people regard themselves as Cotsallers despite the vale laying a lush and fruitful carpet all around the hill. No one knew its secrets better than the late John Moore—let it suffice to say that in his works are to be found the heart and soul of the Cotswold people and the land on which they lived and worked and had their being. An oak tree was planted at the junction of the Bredon road and Westmancote turning as a memorial to him, presented by the Bredon Hill Players: an apt tribute to a great author and countryman whose friendship and encouragement so greatly inspired my own writing ambitions.

We skirt the main Cleeve Hill mass and marvel at man's ingenuity in using these hills. The Dobuni found that defences could be minimized if they camped on a Cotswold promontory such as Nottingham Hill which is rapidly becoming detached from the mass by natural erosion in the same way as Langley Hill separated from it. The depression proved useful to the new road-makers for linking together Cheltenham and Winchcombe.

Cotswold offers a challenge to those who invoke the aid of mechanical power to help slake their thirst for adventure, for here is the universally-known Prescott Hill Climb.

Gretton's pub has personality and purpose, George Osment and his wife, mine hosts of the 'Bugatti', see to that. Catering for all the international races held at Prescott the inn resounds to the excited patter of foreign and native tongues for the locals are not rejected in favour of the visitors: the Continental in his racing gear emitting glamour and petrol sits side by side with the Cotsaller in his 'slop' smelling of the soil and silage. Sing-songs and Christ-

mas parties to which families are taken make the inn a focal point
of the village.

It has also been solemnly spoken of in less convivial surroundings for 'what's in a name' we may quote and the powers that be will
point out the implications. All would have been well if it had
remained the New Inn: the adjective doesn't matter—an inn can
be 'new' forever so it seems (Gloucester's New Inn is a mere 500
years old!) but when Mr Hugh Conway of Rolls Royce unveiled
the inn's new sign proclaiming it the 'Bugatti'—the only one in
the country—the R.D.C. had to set about renaming the lane leading off the main road, for how could there be a New Inn Lane if
there is no New Inn? Parish politics being what they are there was
much hemming and hawing—much of which ran like a mini-serial
in the local papers. All very newsworthy no doubt—but when I
contacted the Cheltenham R.D.C. to find out the latest news on
what seemed such a small point I discovered that although develop-
ers had the right by law to name a street (the right to change a
private or public house rests with the owner) they go to endless
trouble to appease local opinion before changing a name that has
been in existence for some time. Apart from a letter being sent to
each householder in the lane asking for their views, the correct
spelling had to be ascertained. This fact never reaches the public's
notice of course. If you do your job properly that is not news—
if you don't, it is!

Local enquiries brought forth Daglins, Duggins, Duglins, Dog-
lands (being the old route for poachers to take their dogs), a
search through the County archives records it as Duglinch on the
1835 Ordnance Survey map and this is the form the name will
take on a new nameplate soon.

Doug Lynch sounds too much like a T.V. character anyway but
my own bit of dictionary-digging reveals it to be derived from
hlinc meaning rising ground.

And what of the old New Inn whose renaming started it all off?
The brewery has no record of it being anything but the New Inn
but suggested that such a name could have implied that there had
been another inn at the time. And what have the patrons to say?
The 'Bugatti'—New Inn—oh, you mean the 'Rivers Fletchers
Arms'! (But you have to be a local to know that one!)

Gretton's other attraction is its lovely old thatched cottages
which nestle into a cul-de-sac around the deserted church tower.

Pigeons fly in and out the windowless tracery; their deep-throated calls filling the air and their dung fouling the floor.

Another architectural feature in the village is a mansard roof, a most unusual design to find in the Cotswolds. Mr Hurcombe and his wife pointed out many more interesting facets of their house which is named after the fountain erected in 1883 'for the benefit of the poor of Gretton' which used to be fed from a reservoir on the hill before some earth movement cut the flow. A wide window and a kink in the ceiling marked the position of its former role as the village shop. Hand-made nails are all over the house and spikes are still in the chimney from the days when little boys were sent up to sweep the flues. Red tiles were put on the mansard roof in 1906 by the labourers who lodged there while building the railway which, Mr Hurcombe told me with the Cotswold jocosity, is soon to be permanently closed for the second time.

A cottage opposite the 'Bugatti' is reputed to have been a resting place for monks on pilgrimage to Hailes. An old cider mill has gone the way of all old cider mills and remains but a memory of half-drunk wasps winging drowsily through a pungent bitter-sweet past. The village hall proves its former office by 'Boys' and 'Girls' on its back doors, while the old school house wears original shutters on its half-timbered frame.

This old Saxon village was once much larger than it is today as is evidenced by cottage foundations on the outskirts. Like many a village it had footpaths radiating out to take the labourer to his work—Gretton Hill being the short cut to Winchcombe, Green Lane—now overgrown—leading to Langley Hill and Workman's Lane to the jam factory and timber sawmills at Toddington.

The village is proud of its craftsmen and they are proud of their fellow craftsmen. Mr Uedelhoven's thatched summerhouse behind the post office is no longer big enough to house the work of some of the members of the Guild of Gloucestershire Craftsmen; a new showroom has recently been opened and very attractive it is, too.

Pamela Campion had shown me designs in her tiny workroom which she was interpreting for Finley, the Scottish poet, a quite different medium of needlecraft from the tailoring of curtains which she normally undertakes, or the lovely patchwork quilt she had made for a four-poster (for which a step ladder was needed to get into it).

This corner has bred fine needlewomen for centuries. At Sudeley

Castle nearby is a fascinating patchwork bag, the whole measuring
no more than nine inches square composed of 1,537 hexagonals—
a feat for even the accomplished eighteenth-century needle. And
what a tedious task little Jane Badger undertook when she started
picking up the fine threads to stitch "Adam and Eve were formed
of Dust that was their pedigree yet they had a Grant never to
die. . . ." Poor little Jane—such immortality was not her grant and
even the browns and greens of the birds and flowers and Adam and
Eve have faded in the petit point sampler she so carefully worked
at Mrs Tomb's School at Winchcombe.

A sad little story clings to a pair of eighteenth-century knee
buckles preserved also at Sudeley Castle. A wealthy young woman
teased her fiancé, a farmer from Greet, that he was marrying her
for her long purse. The great day arrived and the bride, decked
out in her new knee buckles, was jilted at the church by her
lugubrious lover who sent a message to say he would marry neither
her nor her long purse. The purse, however, was not of sufficient
length. Her veil was parted with for twenty-six shillings when the
lady was old and poor.

I watched Mr Uedelhoven turning local woods—sycamore and
walnut—into bowls while his partner, Mr Campion, was repairing
a fine old chair with the assiduity of the craftsman who had made
it three centuries ago. Two grey parrots and a rhesus monkey
viewed the proceedings, and me, with the equanimity of caged
creatures who tolerate the antics of man at his work. Particularly
handsome were the clock cases so I made off for the old toll house
at Littleworth to see the antiquarian horologist whose work was to
fill them.

Peter Hill's skill is daedal. He makes clocks and any part of a
clock and repairs all kinds of clocks. His tools are laid out with
a surgeon's precision and I could appreciate that such a sudden in-
trusion as mine was as welcome as a Women's Institute outing
through an operating theatre, but with great patience I was introduced to the intricate artistry of horology.

Clocks of all shapes and sizes, variety and value boomed and
chimed, tinkled and whirred, and recorded the while by a small
computer to chart their time-keeping, while I became mesmerized
by the sheer beauty of a chronometer which had measured time
for generations of seafarers since Captain Cook's day. This magnificent horological masterpiece was built to remain stable while a ship

rocked and designed to keep time within two seconds a day. Peter
Hill was justifiably pleased that he had adjusted this one to such
perfection that it gained a mere two seconds in three days. All
ships still have these marine timekeepers—dignified descendants of
John Harrison's 72-pound prototype in 1761 to which he devoted
a lifetime's work to meet Parliament's challenge and prize of
£20,000 to the inventor of a "generally practicable and useful
method of determining longitude at sea."

Just as fascinating were the elegant French carriage clocks also
designed to meet the rigours of a swaying vehicle.

But it is the early English clocks which are Peter Hill's favour-
ite, the finest in the world for over two hundred years until France
and Switzerland overtook us in 1800 with their mass-production
methods. And here, in a workshop no larger than a garden shed,
one of England's few real horologists still makes the kind of clock
—in fact any kind of clock to order—to prove that an English-
made timepiece is still the finest in the world.

Greet is mostly a collection of newly-built houses and I
wondered from which of the old farms the faithless farmer had
sent out his capricious note to the knee-buckled bride in her acorn-
embroidered veil. The jam factory at Park Farm is again but a
memory.

Winchcombe, being a town, will escape our notice now but I
know few will resist its innumerable charms for it was the capital
of the ancient kingdom of Mercia; but we shall be drawn this way
again in a later chapter to seek out the glories of Hailes.

We are at the foot of the escarpment which has by now softened
to a roll of hill along the top of which early man hastened to cross
the 'wild uneven ways' of Cotsall as he headed north. Victorian
travellers skirted the hills by taking to the railway that stretches
into the vale and beyond Shakespeare's Stratford. Today's motorist
is fortunate in having a first-class road running roughly parallel to
the railroad. But the villages in the north-west Cotswolds are unfortunate, one feels, in being so readily accessible to Sir Brum and
his lady who descend upon these 'quaint' little places, the boots of
their Jaguars filled with deep-frozen foods from the Midlands supermarkets so that they need not the services of the village store whose
existence is pure amusement to those who care not enough about
village life to contribute a little towards it.

Tiny Didbrook's church door bears scars from the Wars of the

Roses when Yorkist bullets claimed Lancastrian refugees; its old cottages wear the thatch of vale country and yet 'tis but walking distance from Stanway which is regarded as the gem of the northern Cotswolds.

By far the best way to approach it is from above Guiting quarry past Stumps Cross where footpaths lead off to Lower Goscombe affording almost alpestrine views before the long road snakes down between the trees. One's sense of expectancy heightens as one descends and catches perhaps a glimpse of white doves on a dark thatched roof for there is a feeling that everything about Stanway is that bit more special. A departure from the usual homely village shapes is everywhere.

Stanway House, known to every student of architecture, clamours first for attention. Traditionally ascribed to be the design of Inigo Jones, the gatehouse with its scallop shells draws a quick gasp from the traveller as it stands close to the road for all the world like a grand proscenium. When the sun deepens the stone to a glowing apricot as though the stage-lights are up, artists hasten to match the colour from their ochres and yellows and tawny hues to capture the iridescence, but being accustomed to the softer muted tones of limestone which, no doubt, might seem dull and grey to Stanwayians, I could only appreciate this golden ashlar on such a grandiose scale and found it too obtrusive in cottages. The small church is faced with the same stone and forms a charming group with the great house.

Nearer to my comprehension are the barns of Stanway. Is there a more splendid village hall and theatre than Stanway's Tithe Barn? Famous for its activities and productions it is a treasure of fine stone-tiling supported by cruck frames. A scratch dial on a small stone doorway is some seven hundred years old and evidences its ecclesiastical ties when it served the abbot of Tewkesbury.

Even the war memorial does not conform to the usual stone cross or drinking fountain: Stanway's heroes are commemorated by an outstandingly fine bronze of St George slaying the dragon. Other echoes from the past are perpetuated in a name such as Papermill farm; a sign of good husbandry in faggots of wood stored in the crook of an apple-tree—of such simple sights my heart is gladdened.

By far the most intriguing of Stanway's structures is timbered and thatched and built upon rick staddles like an illustration from a story-book. But it was quite real with a jolly bunch of cricketers breaking for tea.

The pavilion was a gift to the cricket club from Sir James Barrie whom, they agreed, was a cricket fanatic and frequent visitor to The House. They were very proud of the fact that cricket had been played there for over 120 years—I assured them that I would record the rotten score as being their opponents'! (Otherwise they would have diddled the digits before I could take the photo if I know the white-flannelled fraternity!)

It is uniformity and conformity which is Stanton's attraction. Its salvation is due mainly to the architect Sir Philip Stott who bought the estate at the turn of the century and restored it in what we call 'the way it was meant to be' whereas writers asserting their comprehension of our building style will proclaim it 'is in the Cotswold vernacular'. Of course the many gables and steeply-pitched roofs are indigenous to the hills from whence their stone and builders came, perhaps that is why the timbered and thatched North Barn wears an identity disc on its white walls like an evacuee to say that it "was removed here from the Manor House Offenham 1927".

So many of our village churches deserve more mention than I have space to allow them, but as a church is the one place to which a visitor may go uninvited and unquestioned I make no apology for the omission and a wealth of books exist listing in detail the architectural features. The history of a village is invariably preserved in the church and one spends hours deciphering the long epitaphs extolling the virtues of those who could afford to have their virtues extolled while those that couldn't slipped into oblivion—so it was with special delight that I followed Miss Edwards' advice to look out for what must be the tiniest museum in the country. In fact museum seemed a rather grand description for what amounted to a handful of objects. But how evocative that tiny collection of homely things were. A hay-rake, flail, white cotton sunbonnet, a pair of old pattens and a warming pan huddled together as if in a grandparent's attic spoke eloquently enough of summers and winters past. But what a slim lithesome fellow the clerk must have been to nip so readily up those steep winding stone steps when the tiny room above the porch housed the muniments.

The organist and choir are much more comfortably accommodated, for a good wooden staircase leads to their domain. Beneath the oak gallery are pews whose benchends are deeply gouged by the dogchains of those poor creatures who had to suffer the doxologies lauded above and around them while their masters paid respects to their master and listened to the scriptures heaping contempt upon canines. But if the poor old farmdogs became refractory the sermons preached by John Wesley kept the cultured Granvilles, Kirkhams and Izods glued to their pews to stimulate the lively discussions of these young intellectuals of the day.

One can imagine how the conversation ebbed and flowed as the little parties walked and rode through the chestnuts and elms —and did they have the pleasure of seeing the laburnum in its wild golden glory as we do in early summer?

"Inhabitants of all degrees" who had the "right to use the black hearse cloth at funerals without fee" had probably knelt on the old hassocks which were spilling their wood shavings over the floor of the ringing chamber when I peeped in to see the famous ring of six bells, dating from 1640, whose silver tongue can be heard "in summertime on Bredon".

What a fascinating pedigree old furnishings lay claim to and what stories such relics could tell—did the Rector creep stealthily by dark of night with the 'sun of splendour' in a pair of pots to enrich his little church at Stanton with fragments of the former glory of Hailes?

The main attraction of Stanton for me was to meet Mary Osborn who has established a Guildhouse where the old crafts of spinning and dyeing and weaving, stone, pottery, wood and iron work could be practised for sheer personal izzat. My pulse quickened as I climbed above the Mount and saw the house standing solidly on the hillside. It could have been there from the seventeenth century—the classic Cotswold lineage was in every detail giving an artistocratic style to its very simplicity, but the honey colour of the stone as yet ungilded by accretions of gold and silver lichens belied its antiquity. And yet it was that fact alone—that here is a house built as of old overcoming the added impedimenta of eaves gutters, and downspouts, ventilation pipes and other sanitary monstrosities and necessities which cut the face of modern buildings into strips—and raised within the last few years. I felt that Cotswold would perhaps, like the Corn King of old, come to life again.

Miss Osborn is an idealist, but a resolute one—her ambition to set up a permanent centre in the Cotswolds where people of any age, sex, colour, religion, politic or class could work at the kind of crafts which restore human dignity is a noble one fully realized. But because our world is so chaotic and the Guildhouse is known to accommodate those with special needs—be they physical or mental or social, anyone whose traumatic state may be helped by a temporary escape to the peace of the Cotswold countryside in a dignified atmosphere of creative art—there have been some unfortunate attempts to take advantage of Mary Osborn's compassion. I began to appreciate her wish to be left alone to carry on with the work she set out to do.

The story of the Guildhouse began a few years ago when children used to take handfuls of wool they had gathered from the hedgerows to her cottage in Laverton on Saturday mornings to learn the rudiments of spinning. Today, the children of the surrounding villages spin and weave furnishings for the children's room. It was a great thrill to recognize the warm brown and cream of the woven bedcovers as the fleece which the Jacob sheep had worn on my last visit to the nearby Cotswold Farm Park.

The main hall is elegantly furnished with spinning wheels, wicker baskets overflowing with shades of lichen and plants from the countryside, stone and wood delighting the eye and the heart in true proportions. I inhaled the scents of new wood in the workshop as others expand their lungs to ozone. I fingered the magnificent dress and cape of indigo blue which Mary Osborn had spun, dyed, woven, styled and stitched. How good it all was, what fools we are to oust the fruits of the earth from our affections in favour of some inferior imitation of them. Few of us have the eloquence of Rousseau or Thomson or Pope but all must surely understand how

> Sweet is the lore which Nature brings;
> Our meddling intellect
> Mis-shapes the beauteous forms of things: —
> We murder to dissect.

And before passing that by as a poet's fancy penned within a sylvan glade let us remember that Wordsworth had lived a full and involved life in which politics and love and truth and poverty and man's inhumanity to man had each touched him as fully if not more than his contemporaries.

How difficult it is for me to extol the worthiness of this haven in the Cotswolds where one can practise arts and crafts and music not for commercial gain but to realize again that

> One impulse from a vernal wood
> May teach you more of man,
> Of moral evil and of good,
> Than all the sages can

without attracting the curious, but those with a serious enquiry into all aspects of the good life are welcome. And those who despair of such a return to human dignity through the fellowship of others practising the old crafts have only to meet a Mary Osborn to recognize a quiet beauty which only peace of mind can endow.

By way of tiny Laverton, a cluster of seventeenth-century farmhouses, stone-built 'councils' and a hint of a Norman chapel in the stones of a cottage, and so to Buckland, the 'book land' which was held by charter or book by the abbey of Gloucester—a quiet place below wooded hills. The treasures for which lovers of fine art will seek out Buckland church are its rare east window adjudged to be the finest in the Cotswolds and so enrapturing William Morris that he paid for its releading, an exquisitely embroidered Pall five hundred years old and a bridal bowl of great charm and age about which learned men write much. Lovers of quiet ways will seek here the simple charm of the smaller Cotswold village which Broadway the next on our route has lost.

Early man first came to this broad way as the ancient ridgeway took him over the high wolds, and travellers have come to it ever since. Its long street echoed again to the rumble of a stagecoach when it celebrated its millennium. The charter granted by King Edgar, now in the British Museum, is the earliest record of Broadway's existence, and in the way villages are wont to do the whole of its history kaleidoscoped into the fun and frolic of a local affair. Memories were revived and local snippets brought out for an airing to inform the newcomer and remind the native of 'old Broddy' of pre-transport and tourist days. I think it speaks well of the ethos of Broadway to localize the celebrations of their thousand years without succumbing to the temptation of making it a sophisticated national festival.

It was a handful of strangers who resuscitated its crumbling walls to become one of the first of the villages to be 'discovered' and 'restored' at the turn of the century. Since then it has attracted artists and authors and Americans, coach-parties and cafés and clichés. In the main street souvenir shops and modern buildings and tourist trappings are obtrusive while the ancient church within whose shadows old 'Broddy's' sleep is elusive, for about a mile away from the flower-filled streets, tinkling tills and parking problems you will find a village church according to the style of many a Cotswold church. Secluded by yew and holly and sycamore it stands in local stone and solitude. It is not neglected; birds nest and sing and have their being by the leafy hollow through which a stream trickles and cottage flowers brighten many an old mound.

Pretty villages become populous and crowds create commercialism. Again, a cursory glance at a village over the shoulder of other onlookers is bound to distort its true image for here, away from the sightseers, many local crafts and trades are carried on. There are specialist pie-makers and bread home-baked, horology and stone-walling, a cartoonist and a sign-writer, potters and printers, antiques are restored and mosaics are made as well as the famous factory of Gordon Russell Ltd, a firm whose high quality modern furniture has been known throughout the country since 1919.

Fifteen years earlier, Sir Gordon's father, having bought 'The Lygon Arms' and wanting to furnish it with genuine country furniture found it necessary to have a repair shop for his antiques.

At this time Gordon Russell was at school at Chipping Campden. Inspired by the fine craftwork of C. R. Ashbee and his Guild he developed skills of his own, having gained an intimate knowledge of old furniture from his father and sharing with him a contempt for reproductions, he designed a few simple pieces of his own day to go with the older pieces in 'The Lygon Arms'. The early style was closely influenced by Gimson and the brothers Barnsley, artist craftsmen working at the other end of the Cotswolds.

I was told there was no shortage of applications for cabinet making learnerships and I could understand why with such a diversity of pieces on which one could employ one's skill: quite enough to keep two hundred employees busy at Broadway. A perfect compromise between hand-skills and machine-work supplies both domestic and contract markets with woods from the Forest of Dean, native beech and oak supplemented by imported timber.

(*above*) Bourton-on-the-Water has a delightful riparian walk behind the village main street; (*below*) Duntisbourne Rous church through the lych gate

(*above*) Chedworth is charmingly clustered on slopes and shelves;
(*below*) At Shilton—the ford calls for skilful cycling

(*above*) The Cotswold Lion—the sheep which bore England's wealth upon its back; (*below*) Joe Henson—the driving force behind the National Rare Breeds Survival Trust at the Cotswold Farm Park, with 'Trousers', a unique offspring of a belted Galloway with a Gloucester cow

A charming corner at Upper Swell

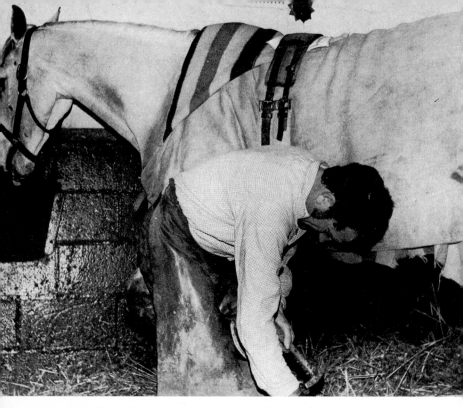

(*above*) Frank Mercer shoes Ann Backhouse's show jumper at the V.W.H. Kennels, Meyseyhampton; (*below*) Ornamental ironwork is wrought at Bill Hall's Barrington forge

WALTER STANLEY PHIPP
JUNE 9TH 1891   NOVEMBER 16TH 1952
FARMER AT REST
ALSO HIS WIFE
ELLEN MARY
MAY 25TH 1887   JANUARY 16TH 1971

(*above*) Wyck Rissington—a farmer's tombstone; (*below*) The house on Wyck Rissington common where Gustav Holst lived while organist of the village church

(*above*) Lunchtime for the woodmen at Farmington Grove; (*below*) Peter and Joy Evans, furniture maker and woodcarver at Whiteway, near Miserden

When the village recently celebrated its millennium it was Gordon Russell's social club who made the pavilions for the medieval markets where Punch punched Judy and gingerbread men went the way of all good gingerbread men—another instance of how important the ties are within a village. And in many a church up and down the land—and across the Atlantic too—there will be found the chair of English oak, perpetuated by the original made by Gordon Russell for Coventry Cathedral, which started life in old Broadway.

The rambler will find Willersey by way of the public footpath which links it to Broadway and Saintbury, and will, perhaps, seek out the steep and narrow byway which comes to the village from the Broadway bend. It is an ancient track and the footsteps of 10,000 years have ground deeply into the hard oolitic limestone. Drawn out either side of a long green the village was 'proper Cotswold' when Massingham wrote his *Wold without End*, but today some of the roofs match the flame-coloured nasturtiums in the gardens.

Parochial life has spread out its pageantry through the homely church and cottages, on the village green and around the duck-pond: history tells us that the manor house was the home of William Roper, son-in-law of Sir Thomas More; contemporary reports inform us that some of the lovely old barns are soon to become converted into dwellings but that the "simple rural farm-like quality" would be retained. We shall see. *Deeds exceed all speech.*

News that was for Willersey's ears only was until quite recent years 'cried' as in days of yore. Until the first world war the Crier, resplendent in hunting pink and top hat, called out to the villagers in the early hours of Christmas morn, "Arise, arise, ye good people arise. Make your plum puddings and your mince pies", followed by a report on the weather and the hour of the day and a reminder "to remember the Crier when he comes round for his Christmas Box". Parish meetings, local events and other important tidings such as "Master Billy's tater-grinder be lost" were relayed in like manner.

One can imagine how excited the villagers became when it was revealed that one of the regular showmen that came to the Willersey Wake to show his kaleidoscope was no ordinary fairground

E

figure but one of the Lascelles who severed his family ties to seek his own fortunes.

Resisting the temptation to be led back on to the hills by Saintbury's slender spire it is interesting to follow the road to seek out the two villages sheltering under the Cotswold edge from which they take their suffix.

Weston-sub-Edge felt the tramp of Roman legions on the near-by Icknield Street, one soldier dropped his spear and others their coins giving proof of their passing. It is difficult to toss the centuries back and reveal again the countryside they knew—for would not the Latins, too, have savoured the drifts of pink and white blossom of the vale lapping the hillside to bloom later in juicy purple succulence.

Keeping faith with the past in an easily comprehended manner is the fine old house 'as big as a little college' where seeds of learning came to fruition under the care of William Latimer. Local historians credit him with the actual building of the house and say the initials W.L. were to be seen carved on the stone- and wood-work. There is still much to be seen today that would have been familiar to this learned and modest man as he preached in the village church nearby.

A rector of Aston-sub-Edge is remembered for 'dying in harness' as we say—the benediction on his lips as he died in his pulpit. Words that live on are those of Herrick paying grateful tribute to Endymion Porter whose patronage to the arts is widely known.

> Let there be patrons, patrons like to thee,
> Brave Porter, poets ne'er will wanting be. . . .

Support to less artistic ventures earned him disapprobation from Parliament and exile from his lovely Cotswold manor with its long gallery the length of the house. But for the compassion of a former servant, an Irish barber, the helping hand would have been stilled much earlier through starvation while in Holland. Porter would be gratified to know that the *Olympicks*, for which he procured the royal left-offs to adorn Robert Dover and 'grace the solemnity', is still an annual, if somewhat modified, event on the lofty hill above the village.

These are echoes from a past, there are plenty of lesser orna-mentations which mark Aston's village life: the loud tick of a clock,

the smell of gas heaters, framed pictures on the wall, chair seats
and pads and curtains stitched from the same roll of cloth—a little
church furnished with parlour pieces; pigs scrumping apples in an
orchard, old cow-sheds, milk churns toppled in a heap, a trickle of
stream through the street—a village of the people.

Burnt Norton takes its name from Norton House of which Mr
Wildgoose in *The Spiritual Quixote* has a moral tale to tell when
the dissolute Sir William Keyte set fire to the house and ended his
frivolous life in the flames. Richard Graves, the author, was born at
Mickleton and bred at Oxford. His father, according to Hearne,
was "a most excellent scholar" an accomplishment which Utrecia
Smith, the curate's daughter, also achieved to such a degree that
Graves and his close friend Shenstone admitted that (notwith-
standing the fact that she was a woman and therefore of an inferior
learning to that of their sex) "she had formed to herself so good a
taste of polite literature and wrote so well in prose" that "a Master
of Arts in the University often said he was afraid to declare his
opinion of any author till he previously knew hers". Shenstone
penned *Ophelia's Urn* to her memory when "that virtuous maid"
was carried off by the smallpox at an early age.

It is difficult to identify "the portico" to which the poet refers
after "snapping up a bit of mutton" at Mickleton and drinking a
dish of tea before making off for Cheltenham. Easier to find is the
fine avenue of elms he planted marching up the slope towards
Kiftsgate Court.

Like the rest of the villages sheltered by the wolds and sun-
kissed by the vale the buildings show deference to both regions:
golden ashlar faces with hoary tiled pates, bricks of blushing pink
and shaggy crops of thatch sport gay aprons of hollyhocks, night-
scented stock and a riot of roses; newly-erected houses hide their
blue breeze-blocked interiors by a veneer of reconstituted creamy
stone emulating that of the hills and wear primly-pruned standard
roses and flowering cherry trees. I noticed, too, the runner beans
ran not, as our do, up wigwam shapes laced together a-top, but up
poles singly, for this is market gardening country. Alas, for the
fruit-and-veg. farmers who had asked for a railway line to run
from Cheltenham to Kineton, passing through Mickleton to transport their produce the faster, aesthetic and commercial needs
conflicted sharply. The vicar at Weston-sub-Edge objected to the
scheme on account of his hymns being drowned by the noise and

local landowners on account of their trees being felled for its passage.

An amenity welcomed by all and accorded a fine memorial is the fountain. The pertinence is no longer so acute, the cause of the monument perhaps forgotten, but the whole is still gay with hanging baskets of geraniums in the summer.

Meon Hill waves a sheep-spangled wooded slope like a flag on the prow of the Cotswold hulk as it dips down into the lushful sea of Shakespeare's country.

To satisfy my own disbelief that the wolds could end I explored the Quintons and Admington but only the College Arms and church wore a stony look—that is if one discounts the diminutive roof so beautifully 'slatted' over a pump in Friday Street. Having "marked well the bulwarks" of the lovely church as bid by the vicar in his leaflet, and giving thanks "for the sun and rain which help the flowers grow" as little Daphne Smith had done in a charming letter left in the children's corner I thought perhaps the well-roofed pump may have been the public one for which a Maria Parker had left money in 1860 to "keep in good repair". The owner of the pump, however, knew nothing of its origin, obviously could care less, and referred to the roof as "a bit of nonsense put on for fun".

What further proof did I need. 'Twas not Cotsall talk, so back to the hills where we build not for fun but for practicability and purpose.

3

Along the Old Salt Ways

BUCKLE STREET: SAINTBURY TO BOURTON-ON-THE-WATER

ANCIENT tracks have been erased over the centuries to crop up in parts as italics on a map. Enclosures and necessity have deflected and deviated our metalled roads to serve traveller and village so for the purpose of following one route marked out by the great traffic in salt, which kept our ancestors in meat during the winter months of the Middle Ages, we can only touch upon the old paths here and there as we follow Buckle Street climbing steeply on to Cotswold through the hedges of Weston-sub-Edge and over the heights of the wolds.

Happily for 'old Reuben', who lives on in the memories of Weston-sub-edge folk, a character who sought work in the cherry orchards and shelter in a deep ditch to keep his independence and out 'of Stow', the rector of his times was cast from a different mould than one of the last century. A casual passer-by would have looked askance at a clergyman scrabbling down into a ditch but to Reuben those surprise gifts of groceries must have been a revelation of the scriptures in an easily assimilated form.

Sweetly sung are the charms of Saintbury, with its slender spire rising out of a sea of green foaming with blossom in springtime to draw the eye ever upward. Visible from every point except the south, the spire seems to pierce the sky so close to the clouds does it appear. I augmented the footsteps of a thousand years to pay homage in the ancient church, the steep steps taking their toll of lung and calf muscles.

No longer do the bell-ringers hurry to the tower on penalty of a fine, for the ring of six bells is unsafe. No doubt, the fees will be decimalized when the belfry rules apply again. A charming homely touch is the group of harmonium players whose faces gaze out of a motley of photographs. I could picture those now bland features hollowed in the lamplight flushing triumphantly as the notes came out with vigour and volume. The harmonium was not the only instrument of music to send its melodies to the lovely Queen Anne roof for William Smith, a dear old white-bearded chappie, is duly accorded a place among the musicians as a bass viol player, a transition from woodwind made necessary when William lost his teeth.

There is much of interest here, not least being the fact that "William Latymer died at his Rectory of Seyntbury and is buried in the Chancel" but the excellent church guide states that the Saintbury rector was not *the* William Latymer martyred in Oxford. That the Saintbury Latymer was a Greek scholar is verified by Wood's *Athenae Oxoniensis* of 1721 in which it says his Greek and Latin books were left to Oxford Colleges adding "yet whether they received them it appears not".

A swiftly gathering dusk pointed the interior with deep shadows which sprang out from between the altar rails like the dogs they were designed to keep out (according to a seventeenth century edict on such matters), the fading light became lost in the lines of a candelabrum wrought of iron by C. R. Ashbee of nearby Chipping Campden so I left the church high on its hillside to its memories and shadows for I had yet to see the rest of this 'burh' of 'swains' from which the village takes its name.

The village clings tenaciously to the hill, its steeply pitched roofs propping up tons of Cotswold stone. Most of the houses belong to the seventeenth century when domestic architecture was at its best and wear the touch of individuality which a twist of the hill or a flowering of an orchard has wrought upon their siting. An old barn stood against the skyline like a wrecked ship, or a prehistoric monster, its ribs dark and skeletal where the stone tiles had been picked cleanly off the fossilized rafters. But I did not fear that such baring of its bones was in preparation of marriage to some incongruous metal sheeting or alien slate, this is a true Cotswold village and wears its ancestry proudly. One inheritance which seems to have been lost happily along the passage of time is the descent of the important Saxon swain who held the manor at Domesday and rejoiced in the name of Hascoit Musard—fortunately neither the name nor its connotations are in evidence today for I saw no dull, lazy open-mouthed fellow loitering around charming Saintbury.

Dover's Hill on the east beckons any day for its view of Meon Hill and every Whitsuntide for the 'Cotswold Olympicks' which have survived the traumas of three and a half centuries. The hill takes its name from Robert Dover who revived the games, with royal consent and patronage, from a Whitsun-ale affair to an event of national importance as a counter to the suppression of old English sports and pastimes. The whole programme of rustic pursuits of wrestling, cudgel and singlestick and cock fighting, bull baiting, dancing and leaping, foot and horse races, quoits and skittles, feasting and wenching filled the pages of Drayton's works with bucolic frolic and puritanical hearts with horror.

Drayton perpetuates Dover's memory with a promise:

> We'll have thy statue in some rock cut out,
> With brave inscriptions garnished about;
> And under written—'Lo! this is the man
> Dover, that first these noble sports began'.
> Lads of the hills and lasses of the vale,
> In many a song and many a merry tale,
> Shall mention thee: and having leave to play
> Unto thy name shall make a holiday.

Prophetic to a point: there is a tablet to Dover on the hill—but none to his grave—the games are held on a bank holiday but under the name of Scuttlebrook Wake, from the Scuttlebrook which once flowed down Campden High Street. Its waters are culverted now but the name lives on. Campden has its own band of Morris men, so the old fertility rites are paced out to the jingle of bells and the brandishing of ribbons. Some of the older sports have been revived but the shin-kickers of old are buried with their peculiar panache and scars.

The Rabelaisian licence which attracted the roughs and toughs from Birmingham, the Black Country and the navvies from the new railroads reached its lowest ebb last century when the powerful rector of Weston-sub-Edge, shocked by what he saw of the 30,000 making merry, succeeded in ending the games by obtaining an act of enclosure for his parish in which the hill lies. It was obviously much easier to end than mend the destructive element. I am sure

the present celebrations would earn the departed rector's approbation.

The Kiftsgate Stone on the Saintbury to Chipping Campden road
marks the meeting place of the hundred's Court but the ancient
seat of British judgement was reticent on one of the most intriguing
of Cotswold mysteries whose gruesome events have been re-
enacted many times as John Masefield's *The Campden Wonder*.
Tragedy took its bitter bite in 1660 at Chipping Campden when
William Harrison, steward of the Campden family, set off to
collect some rents and never returned. Fact and fiction, political
intrigue and simple family jealousies swirl crazily around, clothing
the recondite bare bones with a mystery which deepens the more
one delves.

What ripples of fear and fascination must have generated from
this lovely spot in the Cotswolds as the Perry family were dragged
to the gallows on Broadway Hill still protesting their innocence.
The mother was hanged first as a measure of releasing her sons
from her power and therefore a confession from their lips, for the
days were those of the great witch hunt. Many a spine and con-
science must have pricked as word got around that Harrison had
returned from the other world—not through reincarnation but
with the aid of a silver bowl from a mystic Eastern land. The story
must have kept many a child close to the ingle when a keen upland
wind laughed hollowly in the chimney and shadows leaped with
crooked necks in every dark corner.

No doubt the tale lost nothing by the telling when discussed
in the tiny bar of the old Fish Inn, that quaintly styled pub which
has been cut off the road by the new stretch sweeping the traffic
along from the Five Mile Drive to Broadway. It has a curious style
about its tea-caddy shape with tallet steps leading up two sides
to a weathered oak door. A sundial perched on the top, a creaking
sign of a fish so faded and indistinct as to render it an object of
fancy and a large circle cut into the wall from a hook and chain
swinging aimlessly in the wind makes it look more like a discarded
bit of stage set than a wayside pub. It was bound to have a more
interesting past locked up within its old walls than what regional
books will credit it with—eighteenth-century, they say, full-stop.
But Mrs Burford, the landlady, sated my appetite for the unusual
with a much more gratifying feast culled from ingredients collected by her parents in whose family the inn has been for almost

half a century. The intriguing gazebo-looking part was reckoned to be fourteenth-century and was formerly a priest house. An old charter house inn, it is one of the oldest in the land—its name derived from the sign of three fishes of christianity.

A dip in the ground across what was the old coach road is a hollow memory of the little cottage where former inn-keepers lived and brewed the beer in a huge copper boiler. The old road is deserted now, only a ghostly rattle of chains echoes from the old brewster's house when the moon rides high above the tree tops, sparking flashes off the cars speeding down the hill where ox-eyed daisies clothe the bank in white stars, for today's travellers seek not the simple delights which the old 'Fish' holds.

The wind is rarely still on a Cotswold hill and with such mystery and history to muse upon and the view from over a thousand feet to feast upon, the spirit of the ancient track whispering in every grassy tuft on the wayside, it is not surprising if we regard the circular projections with battlemented turrets as a figment of the imagination as it stands alone in a field like a castle from some gigantic chess set. But Cotswold absorbs such eccentricities quite happily. Visitors have climbed the tower to pit their eyesight against their geographic lore for we are told thirteen counties can be seen from the top on a fine day. The last time I went it was a white cat which had the sole privilege of viewing the vista which had so enraptured William Morris and Burne-Jones that Rossetti's grumblings about the mile-long uphill trek from Broadway with the picnic hampers were entirely lost on them. The tower was built as a shooting box by a former Earl of Coventry after his wife had wished to see if the spot could be seen from her family home near Worcester. A bonfire was lit—the site identified—the foundation stone laid in August 1800. It served a more realistic purpose during the second world war when the top floor made a magnificent observation post and headquarters for the Royal Observer Corps.

As I walked across the open field exciting a gaggle of geese into goose gossip I wondered how long such follies could remain mere vehicles to which we may escape from the madding crowd.

Weary travellers must have welcomed the jumble of roofs set at an angle on the open wolds after the long uphill climb from Middle Hill where crumbling stone walls try to hold the woods back from the road. Snowshill had the mud and dust in their seasons from the old coach road, but has never been defiled by traffic and has learnt the secret of surviving the ravages of an upland winter. Perhaps that is why so many tracks radiate from this high lonely spot on the wolds where sheep on the slopes behind the church give the appearance of snows on the hill even in high summer when hollyhocks are alive with bees.

The manor houses some rare treasures, many of which must have been in use when the surrounding sheep pastures were contributing to the monastic coffers of wealthy Winchcombe. The collection and the restoration of the house to its present attraction are due to the untiring efforts of Charles Paget Wade who presented the entire lot to the National Trust. The nation can now enjoy the culmination of this man's scholarly searches for the interesting. Each room is devoted to a particular subject and all quirks for the curious are catered for: armoury, early bicycles, models of sailing craft and farm waggons, clocks, toys, and all kinds of household utensils, while all the frills and furbelows of fashion's fads and fancies of the past four hundred years form an unparalleled extravaganza. One can imagine how the Mrs Grundys gathered in tight knots in this small hillside village when news got out of Ann Palmer's secret marriage to Anthony Palmer at midnight on St Valentine's Eve in Ann's room, when the vicar, Mr Stone, officiated "contrary to the laws of God and Church".

The old road rides the high wolds past depressions from where stone tiles were born and mounds under which early man lies buried. Lonely windswept fields roll away to infinity, occasionally a huddle of woods chequers the road with shadow while a solitary tree on the distant skyline bows humbly to the omnipotent wind as it scatters abroad the seeds of the giant hogweed.

Geography can be as fascinating to an historian as to a geologist, especially in such an area as the northern Cotswolds where the bordering counties gnaw deeply into the hills. The carving up of the ancient kingdom of Mercia is a good illustration when the old bishopric of Worcester stuck its fork into this particular spot so forming an administrative island in Gloucestershire. Many of these anomalies were ironed out under the Detached Parishes Act of 1844 but Cutsdean across the fields was not surrendered until 1931. What is of interest is the fact that it should remain isolated from its surrounding county for a thousand years—not without question however for a boundary dispute "in the year of our Lord's incarnation 1196 on the morrow of the Nativity of St Mary" brought the sheriffs of the two counties with "many knights and free men" to "perambulate the rightful bounds between the lands and pastures of the townships aforesaid".

What a serious assemblage it must have been that "took oath upon the four gospels" to tell the truth concerning the lands and pastures of Sezincote (belonging to Bruern Abbey but used to belong to David the Priest and formerly the possession of Walter the Deacon) and Teddington (possessed by the church of Tewkesbury). The old deeds make mention of a road leading from Cirencester to Campden and although one cannot now trace its course it is thought to have radiated to the north-eastern Cotswolds from the ancient White Way.

Folks no longer tread out the path of history—all is committed to paper and stored in metal boxes. Memories are fast becoming obsolete machinery; no longer is there the respect for what *they* said. Who those cognizant *they* were has puzzled me all my life. I have sent my elders and betters to near distraction with my 'fussicking about'm' and they sent me to bed supperless and 'right muthered' with their explanation of "They're not nobody it's sommat *they've* allus said"!

An important part of our history which was in danger of being extinguished has been revived alongside this stretch of Buckle Street for at Bemborough Farm, part of an estate owned by Corpus Christi College, Oxford, is the most exciting and worthwhile of all vital work on rare breed survival. Yes, there are lions on these bleak open wolds above Guiting Power, but this is no Safari Park for the lions here are the Cotswold Lions, that aristocratic breed on whose back the wealth of England was borne for so many centuries. It is interesting to find reference to the sheep in the oldest English play *Ralph Roister Doister*—"then will he look as fierce as a Cotssold Lion". Fierce is the last of the humours of a Cotswold Lion, proud, yes, the *noblesse* of the animal kingdom, its Roman nose flaring slightly below the shaggy forelock; traditional Cotswold shepherding leaves it unclipped.

How tempting it is to digress into a long discourse on this ancient breed whose ancestry belongs to the Romans. The inclemency of their conquered land was no doubt combatted by warm cloth from the Roman Longwools—their other famous importation was the stinging nettle to warm up the vanquished! The limestone grew the rich herbage on which the breed flourished so that 'Cotteswold Woolle' was highly sought after both at home and abroad.

Cardinals' robes and royal 'cloths of gold' were made from the lustrous locks and the Woolsack on which the Lord Chancellor sits in the House of Lords originated from the wealth of all England being directly attributable to the trade in wool in the Middle Ages. But this is not a treatise on Cotswold wool—even so, one cannot live in the Cotswolds without being wholly aware of the ancient ties: here a washpool, there a nameplace and everywhere a 'wool church'. The very region is a heritage of the great sheep walks: *cotes* (the shelters in which the sheep were wintered) on the *wolds*, and but for one man, William Garne of Aldsworth 'the great old man of British farming', this noble breed would be but a name to conjure with—as dead as the dodo. The Good Shepherd, in the shape of William Garne, saved a nucleus from which we have two hundred today: a handful, true, but living. A small flock was given to Cranham, so bringing back to that village ancient ties with its former wool-trade. "I did specify that they were strictly *not* to be roasted for the annual Feast, though," Joe Henson, the driving force behind the project, said. The Cotswold Lion is by no means an isolated case, for the whole farm—and true farm it is, no stately home, no zoo, just a typical 1,000-acre farm with sheltered hollows and scattered thorn bushes and wild thyme, scarlet pimpernels, speedwells and eyebright, yarrow, clovers and ragwort—is devoted to the preservation of rare breeds which have played an important part in the development of our own way of life.

Neither is this a secret conservation area of close-meshed wire cages. The animals live freely in wide enclosures, and two years ago the public were invited to share the delights of the open countryside. From Whitsun until the end of September it is the one place where families can go without being chased for money. The picnic area and car-parking and toilet facilities are free; children can limber up on the climbing frames and follow simple pursuits while Dad fills his lungs with the good clean air of 900 feet above sea level.

As Joe showed me round I felt the same kind of awe and privilege and degree of humility one feels on being shown a rare and priceless Old Master which has been miraculously saved from some ignoble fate. Unlike works of art, however, animal life cannot be preserved by putting it behind a glass frame or in the vaults of a strongroom—such is its simple complexity that it must be progenitorial to survive.

At a time when conservation and preservation are brought so much to the fore of public attention it seems incredible that so many species of farm animals nearing extinction fell a long way down the list of priorities. How urgent the problem is would excite an author of science fiction and appal a true countryman. Joe Henson's contribution of foresight, time, energy and cash should be blazoned abroad for, who knows, in tomorrow's over-populated and under-fed world breeds like the prolific Orkney which can live on a storm-lashed seashore and thrive on seaweed may be salvation for some starving country.

Evolution of farm animals is more exciting than concoctions boiled up in a laboratory for what did the Orkney do—when ousted by the English Blackface after the Battle of Culloden—it developed long, black hairy fibres in its short, fine wool coat giving it a mossy appearance to insulate it against snow.

Other northern breeds include the primitive and mouse-coloured Moorit Shetland, the fine-fleeced Improved Shetlands symbolizing the world-famous knitwear—the wool being plucked rather than shorn. I ventured, escorted and within leaping distance of a five-bar gate, to see the yellow-eyed satanical-featured St Kilda ram which had been born on the farm—the last remnant of the extinct Hebridean breed brought over by the old Viking kings. Small brown Soays, whose ancestral remains are found in neolithic graves, showing how little changed the breed is, calls for attention to their antiquity for here is a living example of the first sheep to be domesticated by man.

I have a horn of the White-faced Woodland ram—a magnificent curled shape which would test any sculptor's skill to emulate its delicate waves and ridges and line—the kind of headgear to be appreciated only by another ram, although many a Georgian gent wore a hat from its wool and walked on carpets shorn from its long tail. And here, out of the book of Genesis, is the illustration of the first record of selective breeding when Jacob "took him rods of green poplar and of the hazel and chestnut tree" and by "straking" made them into magic spotted wands and set them into the watering troughs, in the face of which his spotted and speckled and streaked sheep multiplied. No doubt the initial selecting within

Jacob's flock accounts for the great prolificacy of the breed—but commerce laid not such store by the piebalds; coats of many colours were all very well for Joseph in the Holy Land but not on the market stalls of Europe. A nucleus of these ancient animals have been rescued from their most recent role as 'ornamental lawn mowers'.

And how could that gorgeous creature, the Old Gloucester Cow, to whom our early cheese industry and origins of the famous Double Gloucester, be allowed to near extinction? A mere score survive of these beautiful, mahogany-coated dairy cows with their black heads and white tails and docility which earned so much approbation from one of the hunting Dukes of Beaufort that he encouraged his tenants to keep Gloucesters as they "were not disturbed by the passage of hounds". I was introduced to Ella, the proud mother of twin bull calves.

Beatrix Potter would have been in ecstasy over the Gloucester Old Spot piglets who tumbled and squeaked and capered and squealed while their mother nibbled my shoes. Alec the reindeer showed a milder interest in my presence: a close kin of his had died from thoughtless feeding from a visitor's handbag, fatal to this animal which—although indigenous to this country in fact, the rarest and most ancient farm animal in Britain, being the first grazing animal to be domesticated—lives only an dry lichen imported from Iceland. And here is the only prohibitive notice on the whole farm.

Una II, peered from beneath her heavy fringe to look into my camera. Her ancestors were painted on Stone Age caves and Una herself appeared in the national press with her namesake, the actress Una Stubbs, Joe Henson's sister-in-law. A real scene-stealer is Una Longhorn (Mark II), Bardot-fringed, with a proud horny crown, her latest publicity stunt was that of giving birth to a pretty calf in front of the public. Television crews rushed to the spot and organized a competition for naming it.

But Una and Orchid are not the only queens of the animal kingdom: ginger Tamworth pigs had recently made their film debut, routing to camera from a field of brussels; medieval breeds of sheep and goats had just returned from an Arthurian film—even Joe had been dressed up as King Arthur's goatherd. A handsome one at that. Unlike his father, comedian Leslie Henson, and brother Nicky Henson, film star and National Theatre player, Joe's work

is down on the farm. The results are unique, impressive, vital. Con-
servationists are realizing the enormity of the task he has so
nobly undertaken. Sir Peter Scott is very much behind the Rare-
Breeds Survival Trust, which the world-famous naturalist named,
for, as he so rightly said, an aim at survival cannot be classified
under the generalities of preservation and conservation. The two
hundred and fifty breeds are not of curiosity, historical or mere
sentimental value, they are now attracting farmers and breeders
who realize their importance in a changing world.

In the dark dismal days of winter, a farm presents a different
picture from that gilded by summer suns and the battle of survival
on this Cotswold hillside goes on regardless.

How closely entwine thoughts and time; poppies splashed the
stone-dusted banks of Huntsman's Quarry, very like British blood
on Flanders mud and as I passed by methought I heard in the
singing wind of the high road the rhythm of the fox's melancholic
predictions as

> Tom Hill was in the saddle
> One bright November morn
> The echoing glades of Guiting Wood
> Were ringing with his horn. . . .

The ballad, written over a century ago, has a countryman's
heart and soul in its descriptive lines, but the extraordinary pro-
phecies which the author puts into the mouth of an aged fox
"grim and gaunt of limb, with age all silvered o'er" have so far
proved uncannily true. And yet the shrewd pen of this prophetic
poet has not left (as yet) any clue of his true identity. That D. W.
Nash was a keen huntsman who had an intimate knowledge of the
Cotswolds is evidenced by references to places and observation of
rural life. It is remarkable that Mother Shipton is still a legend
and attracts pilgrims to her birthplace when this Cotsaller has
succeeded in going to ground as did the old fox of whom he wrote
—and yet should we not be grateful for that fact alone for which
of our villages might otherwise be accorded the dubious honour of
becoming the 'place of the prophet'?

Villages are resorted to for as many different reasons as there
are visitors to resort to them, and Bourton-on-the-Water must
surely rank as one of the most frequented of our Cotswold villages.
You may look askance at 'village' for it does wear the appearance

of a small town with its wide road and double yellow lines and shops and signs. Beloved by coach party organizers and hated by farm folk is its appalling appellation of 'the Venice of the Cotswolds'. What nonsense. The only boats able to negotiate the low bridges enchancing the green are the ones fashioned from a child's mind and paper bag.

It is undoubtedly a place of exhibitions—butterflies and fish and railway and art and a model of the village itself in the garden of the Old New Inn. This Lilliputian village is a poem in scale and stone—the creation of Mr Morris the landlord who laid its foundations in his vegetable garden as war clouds gathered over Europe for the second time. Only a half dozen men actually worked on the model, which is an exact replica, scaled down to one-ninth, of the village as it was then. The villagers themselves came forward with sizes of their own houses, gardens and displays in the shop windows.

Each building has been built of stone quarried from the hills close by and for those interested in Cotswold architecture, the model can be studied to advantage. The intricate planning took an even more delicate step into the land of Tom Thumb when the garden of the Old New Inn was fashioned for it had to include a model of the Model Village. And included it is—the village again, minimized eighty-one times. The sounds are faithfully reproduced: water falls from the waterfall, voices and organ resound in the parish church, the clock chimes and the mill wheel turns.

It is a great experience to become Gulliver for a while, especially in a place like Bourton, for it makes one aware of all sorts of things not least the viewing of a village in its true perspective. Coming back into reality one can look beyond the coaches and cafés and clothes shops—why a village has to try to compete with the towns as a shopping centre beats me. But the shops at Bourton are 'good' on the whole, and at The Cotswold Shop one can buy chocolates which have been handmade in a Cotsaller's kitchen, local honey potted in Evenlode pottery and fudge, handmade somewhere near Tewkesbury.

It is all too easy to make disparaging remarks on what others do to their villages but I have the feeling that the tenor of village life beats steadily enough to be heard again when 'the season' is over. Bourton is more than a 'pretty shopping place'. Inevitably it attracts outsiders to cash in on the coach parties and the local

(*above*) Children's singing games performed annually on St Peter's Day at Little Rissington, home of the Red Arrows; (*below*) Maypole dancing by pupils of Ampney Crucis school

(*above*) George Swinford at his Filkins 'studio'; (*below*) Chartist bungalow at Minster Lovell

(*above*) A school group from Solihull at work on a practical maths lesson at Burford Wild Life Park: the white rhinos arrived during a dock strike but the dockers made a concession and unloaded them. (*below*) Tree planting to mark Meyseyhampton's school centenary

Nags Head hamlet in the Stroud Valley

names so one finds 'Cotswold' and 'Windrush' heralding all kinds of establishments from perfumeries to laundries. When I attempted to make an appointment to visit the distillery a transatlantic voice sounded highly amused that I should have been under the impression that bluebells may be culled from the local woods. No rural receipts there. All ingredients are imported and processes are zealously guarded—ah, well! I had a good old sniff at the corn sacks at the still working mill.

Further downstream under the hanging branches of a chestnut I found two young Bourtonians, Duncan and Richard, whose knowledge of the Windrush and its muddy hideyholes profited their jamjars to the tune of two 'bullyheads' and three now quite rare crayfish. The village still retains a ford too deep for motors so protecting at least some of its rural character. Here, a tractor bumps along a field where hens fuss and old cottages retain their rainwater butts.

Bourton's history proper precedes the advent of the motor by a few thousand years, certainly the area was well trodden by the Romans whose Salmonsbury Camp was a mere half mile from the present Parish Church where a drain of Roman construction was found, suggesting that the site was once occupied by a Roman temple. The whole area is rich in remains of that occupation. The present-day village was probably too low-lying and marshy in pre-Roman days to be occupied by the neolithic tribes whose camps and barrows stud the higher land around it. Trackways radiate to the ancient sites and it is more than reasonable to suppose that Salmonsbury was an Iron Age 'encampment of a ploughman' utilized by the Roman Second Legion.

Bourton was so named by the farming Saxons without any fuss and bother simply in relation to the camp—burh-tún 'farmstead near the fortification'. Happily, it is only Capricorn on the stone plaque on the modern bridge which brings the links with Roman times to public attention. Tangible fragments are preserved quite rightly in museum cases.

A village of secret alleyways, is the note I made on my pad and I recall walks through the leafiness of spring and frosted autumn stillness alongside the river running its weedy course behind the houses which front on to the 'visitors' river'. The public footpath leads round the backways of cottages with horseshoes over old doors and bundles of kidney beans drying for next year's seed,

F

strings of onions, frayed wicker baskets and the whole miscellanea of a countryman's life hanging on the rough walls. Hawthorn bushes dividing the riparian fields have been coaxed into a leafy archway by generations of villagers, a single stone slab making a footbridge over a drock draining the fields and a wooden kissing gate all serve proper purpose to a country walk where sycamore leaves as large as dinner plates spread a golden carpet at your feet in September and wasps sizzle happily in the windfalls from a gnarled apple tree.

The Manor House possibly sheltered Charles I when he stayed at 'Burton' in 1644 *en route* to Evesham. Sir Thomas Edmonds, being ex-treasurer to the royal household, would most certainly have offered the royal refugee hospitality in his beautiful old house by the Windrush in whose grounds is still to be seen a lovely dove-cote of great antiquity. The manor would have been the ideal hiding place with its secret underground passage to the church crypt.

The King's peregrinations in the Cotswolds are carefully recorded in Manley's diary, the Parsonage being named as another place of refuge in Bourton—the Rev. Thomas Temple having been tutor to the young Prince of Wales.

Smooth trunks of poplars are scored with the loves of the village as the path leads back into the motor-filled street. An echo of earlier transport is wrapped up in the name of the Mousetrap Inn. The landlord told me that it is the only inn name of its kind in the country (there being a Mouseyvaal near a station in Holland) and owes its nomenclature to some Irish navvies who had slipped away from the railroad they were building to have 'a quick one'. The overseer, without too much exercising of his thinking powers, decided that the pub would be a likely place and with great glee pounced on them as they were 'wetting their whistle' saying, "I've caught you in the trap".

There are many aspects of Bourton which makes one forget its selling points—local children quietly hanging Christmas decorations in the wards of the charming stone-built Moore Cottage Hospital, and the birds in paradise at Birdland, the story of which merits a whole book. Suffice it to say that although this is one of the village's major attractions, with each bird exhibiting its foibles like eccentric relations to win affection from the visitors, it is Leonard Hill's early study and love of birds which has culminated in this most exotic of all conservation areas—a very valuable contribution to the Wildlife Fund under the chairmanship of Sir Peter Scott. The fame of Birdland is world-wide and a radio appeal during a shortage of mealworms brought 7,000 bees and seven wasp nests to save the collection of cinnamon-breasted bee-eaters.

Bourton-on-the-Water became prey to news-hungry reporters recently when the villagers were known to have the highest proportion of gout-sufferers. All the age-old remedies were aired publicly and mutters echoed around the hills that since Roman days gout has been attributed to excess dining and wining. Mobile laboratories descended on the village and 'a study' was made. It was agreed that "whilst the good people of Bourton are making a living few of them are in the super-tax bracket". *New Scientist* gently railed the lay Press for its humorous treatment of the news then pointed out that if all else failed there was a patron saint of gout to whom one could pray—St Sebastian, usually shown bristling with arrows. He is, however, also the patron saint of burial societies!

4

The Cotswold Welsh Way

KEMPSFORD TO THE DUNTISBOURNES

ANCIENT tracks marked out by the Dobuni became known as Welsh Ways after the blue-eyed Saxons hunted the old Britons from our wooded wolds. A war of extermination in A.D. 577 scoured the ruins of the great Roman city of Corinium (Cirencester) and the few British Celts who escaped slavery or death at the hands of the relentless pursuers took refuge in the hills of Wales and were called 'Welsh'. It was obviously easier to follow existing tracks than to make new ones so the already well-worn paths of man and animal bit deeper into the land as each generation used them and within living memory the old drovers still brought their cattle along the same routes.

As the mud from the low-lying marshes of Thames Valley was shaken off the travel-worn boots that had tramped up through Wiltshire, the Cotswolds were entered at Kempsford by an important ford of the Thames. A twelfth-century castle, built on an old Saxon earthwork was the home of the Plantagenets in 1298 and remained in that family until the Dissolution.

The village has one of the finest church towers in Gloucestershire—traditionally ascribed to have been built by the great John of Gaunt as a memorial to his first wife Blanche, who brought to their marriage the fame and fortune of the noble Lancasters. High up on the vaulted church roof sixteen red Lancastrian roses are in perpetual bloom. A horseshoe preserved on the church door is said to have been cast from the shoe of Henry Duke of Lancaster's horse as he rode from the village never to return after one of his children had drowned in the ford.

It was here that Geoffrey Chaucer wrote much of his work—
the Lady Blanche of Kempsford being his patroness. One wonders
if he heard the cries of battle when the thin reeds sighed, or saw
twisted shapes in the mists that swirl dizzily beyond the Thames
when he described the plight of the British Celts:

> In all that lond no cristen durste route;
> All cristen folk ben fled fro that countree
> Thurgh pjayenes, that conquereden all boute
> The plages of the North by lond and see
> To Wales fled the christianitee
> Of olde Bretons, dwelling in this ile.

Legend and lore and tales of war must have been zealously
preserved through the ages when one remembers that Chaucer was
writing of an age further removed from his own time than his
is from ours.

Many have been the builders who razed one building on this
site in order to raise another: the castle came down for a large
house to go up by the time the Stuarts were on the throne; the
present Manor Farmhouse was built out of the stables but Buscot
Park farther down the Thames was constructed out of most of the
house stones.

Kempsford has often been dubbed the most haunted place in
England. Certainly the ghosts of all history clamour for attention,
some of them conjured up for me by the quiet voice of the Rev.
Caton whose home had been Kempsford Vicarage for many years.
Accompanied by our steady munching of his wife's lovely scones,
our faces and toes toasted by a friendly log fire, Lady Maud and
the penitent Knight, the little boy in a 'Bubbles' suit, the frightened
lady with her baby and the silent monk were as salamanders in the
leaping flames. But later, returning home alone on the storm-lashed
Welsh Way, the winds whipping the leafless bushes into raging
fiends to ride into the car's searching beam like Dürer's Horsemen
of the Apocalypse—I was thankful for the hum of the engine as
company.

Kempsford must have once been a busy, bustling place. The
characters romping boisterously through the Canterbury Tales may
well have been based on the motley of individuals who added colour
to the medieval market place; the *Calendar of Charter Rolls* records
the village being granted a Friday market as early as 1267 and a

two-day fair each August. Its importance was again realized when the Thames and Severn Canal opened at the end of the nineteenth century, when the long street rumbled to the sound of heavy waggons as sacks of golden grain from the farms of the Fairford area were replaced by coal from the Midlands.

The magic of mystery lingers in the mists of the river; markets and fairs remain but a record, but Kempsford's memories are long as I found to my delight when Cecil King sang songs to me that he had learned at his father's knee. In the little cottage at Reevey which has been his home all his life, he reached a hand up to the ceiling and pointed out where the side of bacon used to be on its wooden rack, and recalled the Christmases of the Mummers. The Kempsford version of which he gave full account, having been part of it for so long, is interesting in having included Morris dancing.

Today, it is the roar of Concorde's mighty engines which vibrate through the village and folks gaze into the skies as Concorde takes their eye above Horcott Hill and into the future.

Even the last of the old drovers who brought their cattle to and from Avebury market on the Wiltshire downs would no longer recognize the wooded and lovely Horcott Hill. The track skirted the edge of Cat's Lodge Woods—one owner going as far as having his keeper's cottage built across what became a public footpath in an attempt to divert the route. Mr Jack Keene, the last tenant of Cat's Lodge, tells me that the locals, exercising their rights and families on traditional Sunday walks continued through his garden —and would have probably gone right through the house to maintain the all-important footpaths.

Such jealous guard of ancient routes eventually succumbed to a greater authority than could be wielded by the old squire's shotgun and Cat's Lodge and the pheasant-filled woods it protected were laid low to make Fairford's famous airbase from where Stirlings and gliders left the green hill for Normandy and Arnhem. The battles of yore hold fascination in their obscurity but to the 'folks who lived on the hill' in the dark days of the war the drone of aircraft at the bottom of their garden was a much more personal thing. The Misses Whiteman whose brother farmed at Totterdown would hurry down the lane to watch for the blinds in the huts to be drawn back. Even after a quarter of a century their voices drop as they recall the thin cheer the boys raised as a mere handful gathered to welcome one another back from D-Day.

Offshoots of the old track went to Dunfield, a quiet hamlet from where the best beef of Rickard's farm came for the market dinners; from 'the famous Hewer's Dudgrove factory' came fine old cheeses. But the Dickensian dinners at the Bull Hotel Fairford were for the farmers and tradesmen. The drovers, among whom only Tiddly Saunders and Chequers—ragged, tough, penniless, sore-footed and hiccuping—have been remembered by name, slaked their thirst at 'The Plough', burnt their tongues on 'Bangham' Barrett's pickled onions, wrestled with the Roman snails he had picked out of the dry stone walls for them and passed a night in the lock-up before making tracks along Sunhill by way of the old Milking Path at the west end of the town close to Fairford's Saxon necropolis. One can imagine what a stir the excavation of the graves caused last century when Saxon skeletons 'one of whom measured a full seven feet' were unearthed with their weapons and beads and pots and armour. The old cattlemen were prey to superstition despite their rough and tough veneer and coins found in Fairford's ford—some even from Roman times—speak of their obeying the custom of appeasing the river gods as they took their cattle through the water.

The road inclines to Sunhill but so gradually that one wonders why it was termed 'hill'. Honeycombe Leaze, a small farmstead and a handful of privately-owned houses, sounds of bygone summers where the bee hives for Fairford's Saxon community stood.

Donkeywell to the east and Betty's Grave to the west tantalize the imagination: the former a couple of houses, old barns, a farm and wide open fields; the latter a grassy mound at a crossroads. And thereby hangs so many tales. Who was Betty and why was she buried at a crossroads?

A suicide? A poisoner? Or is it a witch that lies with a stake driven through her heart? Legend dates the grave as eighteenth-century. The County Records are reticent—the Enclosure Award of 1796 states 'Betty's Grove' which becomes 'Grave' on the first O.S. map of 1830.

I like best the story that Betty took up a wager to cut a field of hay in a day—which, they (again, those important *they*) say she did and was buried at the spot where she died from exhaustion. And so the theories abound—a hooked-nosed hag huddled in black tatters with gnarled fingers clutching a knobbly stick, or a buxom country wench sun-bonnetted with blistered hands from a well-worked scythe? The choice is ours.

The mystery is coloured by the occasional floral tribute—albeit sometimes but a faded plastic spray in a jam-jar—which is placed upon the mound, for the one who pays respect to Betty has never been seen, although houses are nearby. Gypsies? Well maybe; I have noticed that the flowers seem to follow in the wake of the wayfarers.

Akin to the 'diddicoys' was the nomadic spirit of the old drovers and Pop cherished a fragment of one of the songs he had heard them sing in his youth:

> And when we went a-gypsying
> Many a year ago
> When all was dressed up in their best
> Braid and bow from top to toe
> A-danced and sang a jocund song
> Upon the village green
> And nowt but mirth and jollity
> Around us could be seen
>
> And thus we passed the merry time
> Nor thought we of care nor woe
> In the days of our a-gypsing
> Many a year ago.

Cattlemen no longer charm their wards with song, now it is only the motor which hums along the tarmac, although the old knights of the road could have had very little to sing about. No doubt the knot of roofs and chimneys where Akeman Street crossed their path brought a brave whistle to their wind-chapped lips. Ready Token was an old haunt of highwaymen.

Tall trees point the now lovely country house with shadow and legend chequers its aged face with secret. An inn and cottages until 1929, it stands at an important vantage point on the old salt way. I remember being led up to the cross roads on the back of a little brown pony and shivering with delicious horror as my grandfather related the old, old tales of merchants who 'were never seen alive again' after they had gone into the dark depths of the inn. My young mind buzzed with the delights of the quiet spot—the swarm of bees which hung from a tree like a big blob of black treacle, the hangman's stone along the road, being able to jog up to a point as high as Cirencester church tower without climbing a hill and the fact that Grandma was home alive and well after her day at market when others had been slain and buried for their merchandise—and Grandma's basket was always full on market days. But then she went in Mr Dingle's bus. The inn had already been closed many years, but time has no sequence in a child's kaleidoscopic mind: salt-merchants, drovers and cheapjacks, Oliver Cromwell, Queen Victoria and the Black Prince, Shep Tye, King Arthur, and the Romans and evacuees, Hamlet and Noah and Arthur Gibbs, Shakespeare and the 'outride' and Mr Dingle—Grandad spoke of them so frequently that I thought they were personally known to him.

The magic of Ready Token with its chestnut and beech and stone-edged roads that radiate to all points of the compass has never dimmed and was renewed again when Mrs Powell regaled me with tea and more food for thought. Although the inn and cottages are now an attractive house, one of the dogs with peculiar hindsight seemed to know of the former geography and could not be persuaded to go from one wing to where the old inn was. A date gouged into a stone mullion, a knock on the inn door, eight skeletons found in the grounds and evidence of more below the grassy mound and a well so deep that its bottom shows no larger than a penny—fuel for any imaginative flame. I have met those who knew those who had been lowered into the depths of the well 'many moons ago'. And what tales they brought up with them of subterranean passages that would take a horse and cart. It is possible that shafts from the Barnsley stone quarries did penetrate as far as this crossroads.

Folks write of 'strange burials' in the wood nearby. The copse is privately owned by Col. and Mrs Powell and they maintain the grave in accordance with the oath they took when they bought the ground from the Charity Commission, to whom it had been left in perpetuity. Formerly belonging to Poulton Priory, it was chosen by its owner for his last resting place together with his pet dogs. His epitaph requests:

> When I am dead my dearest
> Sing no sad songs for me
> Plant thou no roses at my head
> Nor shady cypress tree

Be the green grass above me
With showers and dewdrops wet
And if thou wilt remember
And if thou wilt forget

Old Man's Beard throws its cobwebby shawl protectively around
the baring shoulders of roadside hedges as the road undulates between the rolling fields to Barnsley. Like most 'street' villages, Barnsley has an inturned look offering no diversion to the motorist to
stop awhile and seek its pleasures. In keeping with those villages,
too, that string their neat stone cottages alongside the road as
though to keep it out of the fields, or the fields from the road, there
is a bend at each end which serves a dual purpose: perhaps originally designed to prevent one end of the village seeing what the
other end was up to, it acts now as a natural check on speeding
traffic.

John Tame, remembered for enriching Fairford Church with the
world-famous set of medieval stained glass windows, passed this
way on his journeys to Rendcombe—fragments of the house which
he built as a half-way rest have been absorbed, it is thought, in
the village pub. Barnsley Park comes from the quarry nearby and
wears its two and a half centuries gracefully. Barnsley House and
most of the cottages are its senior while The Castle's age and origin
remains an enigma.

Changing fashion and needs have made free with the original
plan, now an attractively secluded cottage where I spend Christmas
with friends, its secrets tantalize them and me. Why Castle? Its
site perhaps. The O.S. maps give us no clues. Taylor's map indicates it is Gallows Corner but the perspective and scale of
eighteenth-century maps can be misleading. Bobby and I walk the
field and stop and look and wonder. Are those terraced ridges those
of an ancient vineyard? Why has the barn, whose wall aligns so
perfectly to the house, larger stones in its making? And where is
the oubliette of which Farmer Archer spoke as "somewhere in the
garden". Perhaps it was a monk's hidey-hole or a Roman grain
store—the site of a Roman villa has recently been excavated in the
grounds of Barnsley Park. What secrets our hills do hold!

The Welsh Way, called the Gloster Way on Taylor's map of
1777, climbs steeply across the road into the shadows of a wooded
lane towards the Wold then veers westward past Smith's Covert,

crosses the Fosse Way to Perrott's Brook where the Churn flows shallow enough to serve as a ford before the bridge was built.

It is worth disgressing here to seek out Daglingworth. A history book in stone is this little place folded into the valley: a Roman hand inscribed a dedication to the Mother-goddess, Saxon masons shaped stones into longs and shorts and crude sculpture, the Normans did their bit as one has come to expect, Godstow nuns left behind a splendid dovecote—thought to be the second oldest in the country and still retaining its potence to reach the five hundred nesting holes—a Giles Handcox left his soul to Heaven, love to his friends and to the poor a five pound dole, and Prince Charles who, as Duke of Cornwall, owns most of Daglingworth has recently given £100 towards the village hall improvements fund.

Rural England is here reflected in true simplicity and tradition— one can still see a working forge where the village smithy stands.

It would seem from the old records that many has been the hand that has tried to grasp a piece of Daglingworth: the manor was entailed to William Berkeley by Henry VII and Maurice Berkeley tried to regain the property by lawsuits; then Sir Henry Poole and his son, Sir William, began a period of bartering which ended in a mortgage and eventual split, to be reconciled some thirty years later by Sir Robert Atkyns who bought up the halves and reunited the manor. It was then purchased by Lord Bathurst in the eighteenth century to change hands several times more before it was acquired by the Duchy of Cornwall. Even the Stratton ladies, gleaning in the neighbouring fields, were guilty of poaching "little piles of corn from Daglingworth grounds".

The Duntisbournes cluster and tumble along the shoulder of the valley—a quartet of hamlets through which the babbling brook is a recurring theme. Offering no pretensions to the kind of prettiness which causes their likeness to grace guide books and calendars they charm by their simple congruence. It would be difficult to picture the time of their building, so much a part of the Cotswold scene are their clutch of barns, scatter of old cottages and ancient churches.

A lych gate and saddleback tower are the first clues that it is no simple stone barn that has settled on the steep bank above the brook for the little Saxon church at Duntisbourne Rous asserts no authority in size or style over the neighbouring farm barns. Into the very hillside the old masons carved to set this precious building which has been cared for so well. There is a sundial on the porch and a notice inside says that of the total population of thirty-five, twelve are children and four old-aged—and you envy the few so much.

A small organ like a Victorian piano perpetuates the age-old hymns through its turquoise pipes and the memory of Katherine Mansfield in its dedication. It was a gift from her sisters, one of whom lives in the village and contributes much to its welfare. Craftsmen have stamped the fashion of each age in wood and stone to excite the antiquary, and when one has tired of the flowers of the wall painting and the grotesque heads of the misericords there is a picture of green upon green which cannot be captured in paint or shape if one frames the woods beyond through the tiny slit windows. Fern-edged steps lead down to the crypt from where lichen-carpeted steps lead back up to the chancel. A wild foxglove stood sentinel on top so I didn't explore further. Tombstones floored the crypt, a martin continued its job of cementing rafter to roof and reading desks, carved and redundant, stood in the dark corner.

Some half a mile on, Middle Duntisbourne nestles round a ford, while along the ridge of the hills the cottages of Duntisbourne Leer slope down to the stream which is channelled to run along the road—as though to wash the heels and wheels of travellers approaching Duntisbourne Abbots.

A post office and a youth hostel bring the modern world to the largest of the Duntisbournes where four centuries linger in the shape of a Tudor doorway, gables and mullions, sundials and finials and Georgian windows, and the memory of Old Mac's dog-drawn bread cart. The waters, too, have been tamed to flow into a plant-edged trough, once an amenity and now a focal point on the sloping village green.

The Welsh Way peters out into a maze of tracks and paths which eventually took the cattle to Gloucester and on into Wales. The thin wires of Winstone radio station point out the Roman Ermine Street marching straight as a die to the city and beyond Cotswold.

5

The White Way

CIRENCESTER TO HAILES

So straight does the White Way march out of Cirencester on its northward course that it has often been thought of as a Roman road. No doubt this prehistoric track became straightened out a bit by the Roman villa-owners of the Chedworth and Winchcombe areas who would have used it as an alternative to the Fosse Way when they marketed their corn and wool in the great Corinium emporium. But its course is governed by the ridge of high ground rather than any eye to arterial strategy. Not that the ancient traders were oblivious to the advantages to be gained from a ruler-straight road but they had neither the military power nor laws to protect their trading routes, so densely wooded valley bottoms were places to be traversed as quickly as possible. The medieval salt-traders utilized the same quiet roads and the term 'white way' was applied to this one in particular. 'The Whiteway' leads out of Cirencester to run east of and parallel to the Churn for a few miles.

Baunton, a comely group of church, barn and cottages, is the first village to take advantage of a fold in the hill. It could have been an aged traveller himself who painted St Christopher so boldly in the church. His patron saint dominates the nave, a landscape of trees and churches and windmill curiously insignificant above the dynamic fish-filled waters swirling round his ankles.

The church's other treasure is an exquisite altar frontal of red and yellow embroidered with the rebus of the village name, saints and eagles and all manner of other artistic embellishments. It is amazing how it has withstood the passing of five hundred years and miraculous indeed is its surviving the ignominy of being a cottager's table-cloth!

Manor Farmhouse with its lovely barns perpetuates the etymology of Baunton, 'farmstead associated with Balda', in a more comprehensible manner and the old masons' skill gave it individuality. And here, too, perfectly attuned to the environment is a new house at Baunton Fields. Time's patina has yet to ornament the stone and modern builders bow not to the whim of a mason's fancy—the distinctive facets are in the grounds where Terence McHugh has poured his personality so that his contagious enthusiasm for life and love and laughter exude as much in garden eccentricities as it infects his poetry. One may be forgiven for thinking it was he, perhaps, with his Irish humour that is responsible for his wife's masculine name. But not so. Stuart, his quietly charming wife, has sufficient genealogical fame to account for it, as Charles Dickens, whose chaise-longue graces the drawing-room and family life romps through her writings, is her great grandfather, on whom she is an erudite authority.

The Welsh Way with its wide grass margins crosses our road and dips westwards, but we hurry along the open stretch past Nordown's noble barns and wonder why Rendcomb was built high on the top of a projecting headland rather than nestling cosily into one of the valleys over which it looks. But it is not only its insular siting which gives Rendcomb its singularity, it is as though the architects of all ages descended upon it and wrought their will with all manner of materials. Even the church does not conform to the usual plan and has to be sought out.

It is the college which dominates this village. And what a beautiful site it enjoys, with one of the most enviable of cricket fields.

No trace remains of the original manor which was home to some of the great names of history. Warwick, the 'King-maker', gained it when in royal favour and lost it when he was not; Sir Edmund Tame rebuilt the church and has excited antiquarians ever since into comparing the medieval screenwork and stained glass of this church with that of Fairford's famous heritage. What is of interest is that it was here 'at Protestant Rendcomb' that Sir Edmund the younger chose to be buried rather than 'at Romish

Fairford', where both his grandfather and father lie in great state beneath bold and beautiful memorial brasses.

The Guises are remembered for the superb Norman font—and the family's "hereditary worth by active virtue and by the parliamentary confidence of the county of Gloucester". One such activity which tests our credulity is the record of Sir John's duel which took place at Perrott's (then Barrow's) Brook when "Sir Robert Atkyns, the county's historian, run him through the body—the sword going in at his navel and coming out of his backbone, he falling at the same time into a sawpit, and the sword breaking in his body". That he lived to fight another day is as remarkable as the thought of the curly-wigged Atkyns engaged in such a fracas with one of the landed gentry about whom he wrote so ingratiatingly.

Many are the tracks that converge on Chedworth, twisted, wooded ways to enchant the walker and infuriate the hasty. It is no place for the rabid road-hog who would be distressed to find himself looking up to a doorstep and down on a chimney. The rambler will find it by way of Shawswell through Kennel Bottom; and older people will remember old cottages up the valley where there are woods now.

Following the White Way as it passes secretly through the woods one can sympathize with the old character who had celebrated Christmas rather heartily and prematurely and found himself alone in Chedworth Woods in the darkness of night and 'mugglement' of drink. Despairing of ever getting home he kept up a call of "Man lost". An owl repeatedly replied in the way owls are wont to do, which to the man's befuddled ears sounded like, "Are you? Who are you?"

"I kips telling on-ya, ya dalled ol' fool 'tis ol' Jack o' Chedoth of course."

But not all old tales of village life raise a smile. I came across one in the County Records Office—an inventory of a Chedworth pauper's home such as would have set William Cobbett a-gallop and his pen a-pace: one bed and two little barrels, one iron pot, two wooden tubs and a "litel cetel [kettle], one coberd, one corfer, one table, one bucket, one frin pan, one binch, one fir shul [fire shovel], one pear of tongs, a pear of bellis and a pear of And Irns [handirons]." Poor Ann Coates, the Chedworth homes of today bear little resemblance to your poor hovel!

Social circumstances change but not a craftsman's skill. One tends to venerate the artisans of old with never a thought for those who restore and patch and preserve their work. "They can't do that sort of work today," pronounce the pessimists (or those who care not enough to seek out those who can!) and one fears an artless future when time has finally taken its toll. I am as guilty as any in referring to the 'old masons' when, in fact, one really means the masons of old, but here, at Chedworth, is a young mason very much a part of today's world whose stone carving is every bit as beautiful as that of the medieval mason's.

If Peter Juggins had a *pied à terre* in Chelsea, or whichever district is currently fashionable for artists, patrons would be beating a path to his door and his work would glow in softly diffused light at smart exhibitions. Happily, for the good of our Cotswold heritage, his studio is a very unobtrusive and practical workshed where huge blocks of Clipsham stone become exquisitely carved church pinnacles. I marvelled at his ability to discern the original pattern from the mass of broken masonry lying on the grass—a dozen or so pinnacles which had been swept off Fairford Church in a hurricane. Five hundred years had gnawed deeply into the grey stone, gold and orange lichens were so fossilized as to distort the outlines drastically but with the inherent understanding these 'men of stone' have, Peter interpreted the pits and oddly-shaped bumps and using the same kind of tools as the masons used when they built the church in the time of Henry VII he transformed the inanimate white block into a thing of beauty. Foliage and fruit emerged, crisp yet fluid, stark yet subtle, to the magical ring of iron against stone. A veil of white dust covered chisels, bolsters, files, claw marker drags, banker: a Madonna of fine open-grained Weldon stone looked down on the proceedings and I realized yet again what a fascinating commodity stone is; its formation, characteristics, uses and the masons who work it warrant a weighty tome. Like most stone carvers, Peter makes his own bell-shaped mallets from apple, holly or yew.

His own intense interest in, and feeling for, stone was manifested later as he introduced me to the village as only one born and bred to a place can. Local history is suddenly brought to life in human terms. And there is much in Chedworth to set even the most dormant of our antiquarian instincts twitching: a church window in the stables of the Manor House, a cobblestoned dip

(*above*) Donnington Brewery on the Dikler. (*below*) Young anglers at Lower Slaughter mill

(*above*) Widford's ancient church stands alone in a field. St Oswald's funeral cortège may have rested here on the way to Gloucester; (*left*) Double row of beakheads arched over Windrush church door

(*above*) Sheephill Barn on the Roman Akeman Road above the Leach Valley; (*below*) Barn at Naunton

(*above*) Mr Stallworthy, one of Cotswold's last millers at his Ampney mill. (*below*) Keble Bridge links the Eastleaches

leaving a picturesque memorial to pre-piped days. Many a salt-dealer must have walked down those cobbles after he paid toll to the royal manor of Chedworth; the wooden tithe barn which stood close by has also been transported to the land of long ago. Most of what makes up a village has a pedigree: the stones of the churchyard path were elevated from the stables by the 'Seven Tuns'; an old stone in the church porch probably came from a more ancient one. The local name of St John's Ashes possibly refers to the site of the Preceptory of the Knights Templars—ash trees colonize well on quarried ground—and those who know a ragstone from a cut stone will detect which of those in the field wall some quarter of a mile away once served a less menial purpose. The Latin inscription on one of the south buttresses to a Richard Sely indicates that his wife's bones were removed from elsewhere to lie in his tomb, this would perhaps imply that she had been buried in the earlier church.

Who the Richard Sely was is left to conjecture. That he was a steward to Neville the infamous Kingmaker, whose family owned the manor, has been suggested. That he was a benefactor is likely; the fifteenth-century windows are unusually fine for a church of this size and a popular endowment of the wealthy wool-merchants of that period. What is of peculiar interest is the employment of Arabic numerals in his inscription and the lone 1485—the year of the Battle of Bosworth—on the turret face. One can imagine the 'oondermenting' that went on as the mason carved those! No doubt such importations introduced to our hills from the inter-national wool-buyers would have been a novelty to the villagers, and a bit of 'one-upmanship' for Chedworth. And what a great day it must have been for this quiet valley when Elizabeth of York paid it a visit, no doubt her avaricious young spouse waited eagerly for her report on how his newly-attained manor was faring. The royal Tudors are thought to be represented by corbel heads inside the church, while the honour is preserved in the name of Queen Street.

The continuity of craftsmanship is perhaps more vividly illus-trated in church architecture than in any other tangible form: the intricate stone carving which Peter Juggins had recently executed was so perfectly attuned to the old stonework that it is only time's hoary patina which showed those parts that had stood for over a half a millennium. Here also, was the first example I had seen of a stone patch! Such a domestic touch as a neat patch in a table tomb called for exactitude on someone's part, a point appreciated perhaps by only another stonemason.

Appreciation of other craftsmen's work is leavened by local pride and an artist's eye for detail. The brass almsdish with the Good Shepherd bordered by acorns, the work of another Chedworth man, Denis Keen; the classic lines of the Madonna sculptured by Helen Frazer Rock, the contemporary Trinity frontal, vibrant in colour and line, the design of Andrian Shaw a local art student; climbing the circular staircase to where the roodloft once stood to run a finger over the delicate tracery forming a turret window, disentangling 'Andreas' from the patchwork fragments of old glass in a chancel window, scanning the walls for masons' marks, recognizing that the fifteenth-century pulpit was executed from one block of stone and why the carving was not completed and the base doesn't exactly match the wineglass stem, all telescoped into a fascinating whole in which time is irrelevant. On such a *vade mecum* of the village the sundial's motto that *Hora brevis vitae* is an apt message.

Chedworth is laced together by old tracks, a story to be told along each: Ballingers Row where the weavers of old eked out a meagre livelihood to be lightened by the lovely view, the strain of the undulating valley roads on the waggon horses shown on the inn sign where the drivers once stopped, Woolpack, Hawk's Lane, Gallows Lane, Kite and Coffin Grounds, a washpool, a trough in Calves Hill, hurdles being made by Ted Pearce, memories of the Pickwickian cobbler with a mouthful of nails, bread-baskets in the window and tallet steps to Day's the baker, the cruciform shaped Old Farm, windows of four different levels in the farmhouse up Cook's Hill, dips and hollows where stones have been dug for houses, the quarry proper from which the runway of the airfield was built for the last war, the railway cutting deeply through the combe, are names and scenes to conjure with while walking some of Chedworth's seventy-four footpaths. No doubt at least one of those was created to allow the villagers to catch the train that rattled through their fertile dell—they having to walk initially to Fosse Cross, some two miles away, to board it!

After I left Smuggs Barn, a former inn with its own goodly store of antiquity and tales to tell, a cheery fire and good friends, the legends of old took on a new form as I passed Chedworth Beacon—in signalling line with Ready Token. Traffickers carried other commodities beside salt along our 'rough, uneven ways', the round barrow in the woods obviously made as good a hiding place for contraband from the Bristol ports as table-tombs did for the local poachers' catch!

Who knows, "brandy for the parson" may have more than a ring of truth in its telling: in a very fine first edition of Atkyn's *History of Gloucestershire* a Mr Snell of Guiting Grange made a carefully inked note in the margin against Chedworth that "by custom, the inhabitants of this parish claimed the right to be treated by the vicar to free bread, cheese and ale every Christmas Day". Subtle blackmail? We shall never know, but the present vicar, the Rev. Arthur Dodds, is only too happy to find his parishioners do not insist upon their ancient rights—especially as he takes such an active part in village life to the extent of occasionally helping to serve at the Seven Tuns Inn!

To return to the White Way we take the road through the woods deep in shadow. Is there any more depressing place than a disused airfield—ghost towns of Nissen huts and weedy tarmac, the haunt of owls, pigs and learner motorists.

The road rises to fall again into Compton Abdale, a place of running water. A low stone edge channels running water neatly down the sloping road through the village. The spring at the bottom must have refreshed many a dusty traveller long before the stone crocodile was born. No longer the amenity it was, the creature looks as though it has escaped from the company of the animals on the church buttress, but moss and fungi give it a strange prehistoric appearance. The weeping willow nearby serves as an admirable notice board for local events.

Local people cross the A40 with care, not only in deference to its being a busy road but strange and unexplained accidents have been attributed to the restless spirit of a highwayman who once forced stage-coaches off the road. Certainly on a quiet evening when heavy clouds race each other across the undulating wolds the Puesdown Inn is a welcome break on this high sweeping road. But we head northward. No doubt the handful of folk who lived in Hazleton were the first to hear of the goings-on and were glad that their comely group of big house, farmsteads and church sheltered so snugly into a fold of the hills.

Tumuli stud the way to Salperton and we are reminded yet again that the loud trumpet of war reached as deeply into the hollows of the wolds as it did through city streets: this small village could have ill-afforded to lose so many from its few.

Hawling makes another pleasant diversion and one is constantly amazed at the diversity of sites the men of old chose to wrest a living from the soil, to raise a house, a church, a manor and develop them into a village. The stone warms quickly to the sun and one is aware that there is still space to breathe in this small island of ours, with only a cloud shadow to break up the pattern of the rolling landscape.

The road Lord Chandos and his family took while the Round-heads made free with his castle at Sudeley crosses ours at Roel Gate—a bleak high spot. The remains of a chapel at Roel Farm to the right which gave them shelter echo of greater days, and the suggestion has been made that it is the site of a vanished village. The stone bench at Roel Gate crossroads would have been a wel-come seat in days gone by, perhaps not quite as necessary today but a pleasant memorial to Arthur Boycott 'Pathologist, Naturalist and Friend', where one can sit with only the wind for company and watch the sun setting beyond a wide shoulder of the wolds, with crows on the backs of sheep making strange shapes against the fading light.

The whiteness of newly quarried stone makes luminous patches in the weathered walls of Sudeley Park as they guide the road across Salter's Hill into Salter's Lane to leave the Cotswolds at Hailes and so northward to Droitwich.

The compulsive beauty of the Abbey ruins has drawn even more pilgrims to Hailes to augment the tracks worn low by the devotees of old. Oft has the tale of Hailes been told: it belongs to England's chequered past.

All is quiet and peaceful in this little hamlet today, an occasional busload of sightseers gaze solemnly up at the chapter house arches and down into the deep walled drain and read off in hushed whis-pers the labels from the ragged walls: cloister, dorter, frater, warming house, undercroft, reredorter, transept, vestry; like ancient charms the names run together like a scrap of poetry. There is a natural tranquility about the place that demands respect. Sometimes you can be the only soul to wander at will through the ruins, the lush close-clipped grass hushing even your footsteps, the guidebook of the Department of the Environment to fill in the background and your sense of history conjuring up the pageantry—

it is the stage on which to let your imagination run riot. But even if there are scores of visitors there it can help one to appreciate scale; a hundred people won't crowd the area of the chapter house.

What an upheaval to this little hamlet the arrival of the masons, carpenters, tilers and labourers must have caused. The castle was already but a dim memory and a decayed ghost of its former self. The hill ringing to the sound of iron upon stone, groaning waggons, straining horses and falling trees must have kept the little community agog. Then to the great abbey which rose up amidst the rubble and dust and mud came the King and Queen of England, many nobles, thirteen bishops and three hundred soldiers and, of course, the man whose promise was fulfilled—Richard, Earl of Cornwall, for it was as a thanksgiving token for the sparing of his life at sea that the abbey was built. What a romantic figure he must have appeared to the handful of peasants—the King of the Romans himself. After the grandeur of the dedication service was over and the royal procession had left the secluded place to the white monks and the woods, the great job of cultivating the land around it had to begin. Even today, the well-fed, warmly-clad visitor can find Hailes a bleak spot despite its cloak of dark trees; to the monks, hardened as they were to an austere life, tilling of the heavy clay must have been a formidable task.

Like most monastic communities, Hailes relied on its sheep, manor rents and appropriation of surrounding village churches for its income, but plague and poverty took its toll and rents were difficult to collect: the manor of Lechlade, for instance, became a financial burden rather than an asset; the great Earl could have little realized the impracticability of endowing the abbey with a parish in the south-eastern corner of the Cotswolds. No doubt the rent-collector made use of the branch of the saltway that can be traced just above Compton Abdale to run south-eastwards along the A40 to Hangman's Stone, dropping across the Fosse Way above Stowell Park to run by Crickley Barrow, past Saltway Farm through Coln St Aldwyns by Barrow Elm to Little Lemhill (old Haymill) and so into Lechlade and the start of the navigable Thames; a pleasant enough trip today but a test of endurance in the thirteenth century when only rumour and bad news could traverse the bad roads quickly.

Perhaps the countryfolk never quite understood why Earl Richard was King and his wife Queen of the Romans, but they doubtless recognized it to be a great honour, and although the final achievement of becoming Emperor and Empress of the Holy Roman Empire was never to be theirs, the fame of the abbey they founded at Hailes was to rise to great heights. Their son's presentation of the Holy Blood drew the greatest of noblemen and the humblest of monks along the leafy tracks to pay homage at the shrine and fill the abbey coffers with untold riches.

But the reign of a later Henry was to bring visitors of a different ilk to the abbey doors: the bells rang out for the last time on Christmas Eve 1539; lead was torn from its roof, most of its stones and tiles scattered or pilfered to enrich the great houses around; the precious phial was discredited and held to ridicule. Hailes had fallen. Unlike the townsfolk of Tewkesbury who could raise enough funds to purchase the abbey church as their own, Hailes had but a handful of cottagers who had their own parish church anyway.

In a strange sort of way this little homely pile, set in a field with a backcloth of dark trees making a perfect foil to the mellowed stone, embodies a somewhat deeper religious dignity than the stately skeleton across the narrow lane. The damp smell of dry rot pervades the air, the colours of the wall paintings have lost their vibrance and the cartoon-like shape of three long-nosed dogs leaping at a sleeping hare beneath a tree with huntsmen in the background strike a comic note as though the villagers decorated the walls with any flights of fancy in an attempt to make this humble church a gay opposite of the solemn abbey. Tiles with heraldic devices scrounged from the abbey are haphazardly inserted in the floor. All is so quiet that it is possible to hear what could be rats gnawing at the ancient panelling. It is a lovely place and wears its antiquity with grace, after all, it was already a centenarian before the abbey was conceived.

Sudeley Castle to the west warrants a long visit and merits its own book. Even then it would be impossible to absorb the thousand years' history—curious, fascinating fabric into which the lives of the most colourful of our royal kings and queens are interwoven. The Castle, gardens and exhibitions are open to the public; to name but a few of the delights would be indiscriminate.

Services are still held in the parish church of Sudeley which was used as a stable for Cromwell's cavalry. Queen Katherine Parr's funeral was an auspicious occasion carried out in the new faith when the black-draped chapel heard the English tongue for the first time, and yet her resting place seemed to have been forgotten for over two centuries. The present tomb was erected by the Dents last century. It is to that family, whose home it still is, that the restoration of the castle and chapel is due.

Emma Dent was a tireless and generous benefactor to Sudeley and Winchcombe, not least among her contributions was the diversion of water from St Kenelm's Well to Winchcombe in 1897. Her obituary gives a glimpse of her indefatigable activities, among which her scholarship and love of the area is evident in her annals, and that she cared not only for buildings but also for people is shown by a little entry, "she always employed local labour where-ever possible".

To her untiring efforts is owed the magnificent collections where time's magnanimity has placed Oliver Cromwell's inkwell along-side a silver memento and mourning ring of Charles I.

The most dormant of our senses for history will be stirred by Sudeley—even George III 'came to look' (and fell down a staircase!), and no one escapes its lure: the engineer, Mr Tom Ferguson-Elliott, tries out the medieval recipes he is collecting and cooks pigeons with gooseberries down in the castle kitchen.

History goes underground, too, in this corner of the Cotswolds. The Romans of Wadfield were as curious as we are it would seem, although from the potsherds and bone scoop and coins (now in Cheltenham College Museum) found inside the entrance it would seem that the neolithic long barrow provided an elevated spot for a picnic and an idle hour for gambling rather than a place of morbid curiosity. Certainly, the prudent Saxons found some of the Cotswold barrows ideal shepherds' huts! The official notices say-ing it is an ancient monument bring visitors to Belas Knap with more respectful motive. What is heartening in this expendable world is to recognize in the dry stone walling the same principle which governs the waller's craft today, a human skill which has laced together four thousand years in our native stone. From Belas Knap, above Humblebee How, the hills stretch from sky to sky and man can be as alone as Adam.

In the next valley lies Postlip, beautiful, secluded and historic. Industry would sound a sacrilegious word when applied to this entrancing valley, but the natural abundance of pure water pro-vided power for mills as well as deciding a site for a village. The Norman auditors noted two watermills at Postlip and would be surprised to find one still there—not the same, of course, but the northward flow of the Isbourne is as vital to today's production methods as it was for powering the waterwheel. An old Cotswold saying that water which runs against the sun is bound to have peculiar powers would seem to be a valid observation, for it is the total absence of iron in this water which ensures the highest quality filter papers to be made here.

The firm of Evans Adlerd celebrated its bi-centenary in 1947. Its history is a chronicle of happy relationship between the owners and the workpeople. Waggons loaded with rags have been replaced by modern transport bringing wood pulp from Tunisia and Sweden, America and Finland. Some sixty tons of all types of absorbent and filter papers leave this lovely spot for the home and overseas markets every week. There can be no better example than Postlip where industry can be made a local amenity—a means of livelihood for almost two hundred people—while not detracting one iota from the charm of its rural situation.

The history of the firm goes deep into the heart of the Postlip valley to one of the finest Elizabethan country mansions in the Cotswolds. Postlip Hall's own tale would take too long in the telling, its architectural features have been so often published, its enigma alluring, its siting enchanting. Houses of such age and dimensions face uncertain futures; proposals invite speculation and any enterprise attracts investigation. When a group of four families bought the mansion, tithe barn, chapel and the fifteen acres they stand on as a joint venture even the television reporters got interested. But they were disappointed—the families, now six, lead their own professional lives in their own 'house': no communal living; no food for news-hungry reporters. The group formed a Postlip Society and use the beautiful tithe barn as a cultural centre. The acoustics are remarkably good, and artists of international repute are invited to give performances. The society, whose members are drawn from all corners of the professional and artistic fields, is very discriminating in its programmes. Only the first class of its kind is ever presented—poetry, music, visual arts, drama— we recognize those whose task it is to budget these events by their perplexed air and nibbled down fingers!

Coming home, back along the old White Way, after a Twelfth Night party with log fires blazing in the cavernous hearths; a ramble through the bluebell woods, an intoxicating evening of music, or an animated conversation with John Wilkinson and his wife, whose violin may be hanging above our heads in the throes of being restrung while we down enormous mugs of coffee in the kitchen, I know that Postlip's most memorable chapter is being written in the twentieth century.

6

The Roman Fosse Way

CIRENCESTER TO LITTLETON DREW
CIRENCESTER TO DORN

This Roman road runs straight and bare
As a pale parting line in hair

'SCRATCH Gloucestershire and find Rome'. But it lies now in the Corinium Museum. Each summer's 'dig' brings a little more of this capital of *Brittannia Prima* to the museum cases for modern Circencester to expand over the ancient foundations with impunity. It is impossible to look at this developing market town where modern supermarkets share the same pavement as a saddle-maker's, where in the market place at canvas-topped stalls, gentle 'county' voices still trip over the decimal prices of W.I. jams and pickles, and imagine the classic temples and public buildings of Corinium. But under the expert guidance of Mr David Viner, curator of the town's museum, the fragments of the past fall quickly into place and one begins to understand the audacity, the administration and the enormity of the task in imposing a highly developed civilization on our woad-daubed Dobuni.

Voltaire once said that the Greek and Roman governments are the subject of every conversation. Latin lingers in lapidary inscriptions, and medical prescriptions but we are as free as our nomadic forbears to go hither and thither as fancy dictates to find out what we have made of the Cotswolds since the Roman legions tramped these straight-as-a-die roads.

For the purpose of finding our villages we must, as I say, follow our fancy; the line drawn on a map as the Fosse Way will guide us, but not dictate our every move for it links but few villages or farms and, except for traffic, can be as lonely as the old trackways we have followed. The canny Anglo-Saxons who named this road the Fosse Way, on account of its having a 'fosse' or ditch on either side, tended to settle off the Roman roads which would have left them vulnerable to surprise attack.

The straightness of the road is immediately signalled by the speed of the traffic as it leaves the town south-westwards. Old Father Thames looks benignly down from a sign inviting the thirsty to stop at the Thames Head Inn, and the curious and the patriotic to find their way across the fields to where *O Tamesine Pater* reclines stiffly in stone like some Greek god—a rather pompous patriarch to equate with the feeble embryo of the Thames. Sighing trees, bird-song and the soft roll of the Cotswold tongue as farm-folk tend their cattle are the sounds one hears in this quiet spot— no gushing water. Only after a heavy rainfall does one even see a puddle, the water running underground before it asserts itself.

Kemble, for all its other charms, means a country railway station—an ever-vanishing amenity from our region. Tweedy gents with hampers and grey-flannel-suited young ladies with public-school accents and bright-faced young executives with rolled umbrellas converge on its platform—like the Thames, it is an artery to the city. The G.W.R. clock on the 'down' platform has gone the way all old railway mementoes have gone. The modern British Rail design on the 'up' line has no appeal to collectors!

What vicissitudes the trains have run through! What powers the squirarchy had! Kemble's squire stamps through the records as an irascible scamp, making so many demands on the company that it is a wonder there was a line built at all. Obeying his command, we hurtle through a tunnel almost 500 yards long in order not to be seen from his residence.

The Fosse Way can be rejoined just above Jackaments Bottom to become an indiscernible track across fields—a delight for riders and walkers.

Culkerton no longer vibrates to the rattle of trains: the station house is a private dwelling and marigolds stud a smooth lawn with golden stars where the track once shone like strips of licked liquorice. Even this tiny hamlet was not overlooked by the Domesday compilers whose countrymen chose to build a church at Ashley close by.

The observant will spot the *agger* of the Roman road at Long Newnton and we feel the ghosts of the Estcourts calling us on to see them at their devotions at Shipton Moyne. The church, no doubt, is held close enough to the villagers' hearts for they enter it under all the trials and triumphs and tribulations of life but I would feel strangely alien and prohibited in such company, an illusion emphasized by the shadowy figures at prayer, the Estcourts have been so engaged for six-and-a-half centuries, their presence fills the church in awesome effigies. No doubt the great Renaissance monument is well thought of for its splendour, but painted stone always jars my primitive senses. Little Elizabethan figures in ruffs kneel round the tomb-chest like a frill on a birthday cake. What a polyglot message the monumental masons imparted in their work—armorial bearings, skulls and crossed bones and swags of fruit.

One feels that the squirarchy was venerated more than the deity by the Victorians who practically rebuilt the church. But death is the leveller: the bones of the lord and the carter, lady and kitchen-maid lie side by side in the well-cared-for churchyard. What a quiet place it is. I went on a Saturday morning and saw no one on the streets, the inn-sign of the 'Cat and Custard Pot' creaked eerily and a playful breeze clanged the school bell.

Easton Grey belongs to Wiltshire and the valley of the Avon which so delighted the dour old Radical, William Cobbett, that he sat upon his horse and looked at it for half an hour, though he "had not breakfasted". But its bones are Cotswold.

The church accords readily to my conception of a village church. The high pews suggested illicit games of noughts and crosses for bored youngsters, especially in the cosy privacy of the boxed pews, but church furniture designers seem to have thought of everything, the canopied Jacobean pulpit is high enough to allow the vicar full view of his flock. No excuse for mutterings and mumblings over the Creed and Lord's Prayer either, here they are in bold lettering framed on the white-washed walls, and the Ten Commandments to keep one on the straight and narrow. The grandest thing about this quite lovely place is the name of its attacker, *Anobium punctatum*, the little pest that peppers the woodwork with flight holes. But its days are limited, it is doomed to share the fate of the death watch beetle whose antics in the belfry have been dealt with.

If Cobbet rode his rural rides today he would be hard put to to find a swine-herd in or out of 'the stubbles' to lead his horse down the muddy steep. The hills do not present the same problem now, of course, as they did when he jogged his way to them. I qualify *to* them and not *down* them for he seems to have been an irresolute horseman when faced with a tricky descent. But his racy pen would find little to put on paper, unless he became disposed to praise that homogeneous tumble of roof and bridge and wall and house and church and cottage we call a village, built of the stone we love and he loathed.

Old-fashioned weights are still used at the diminutive Post Office where a very nice lady showed me a stone-built cave affair which the old people had used as their communal larder. Snow and ice were thrown into it during the winter which by some natural means insulated it sufficiently to act as a cold store in the summer.

At Pinkney, another charming spot where the Avon is a centre piece in a delightfully weedy, natural way, Berowald Innes carries out the highly specialized craft of heraldic embroidery. A fascinating wall frieze depicting the Armorial Bearings of the Innes family since 1160 illustrated the patience and skill of 500 hours working 160,000 petit point stitches.

At Sherston, history is captured in a different medium. Mrs Stancombe specializes in painting first-day stamp covers. The philatelic range extends from the Dickens centenary collection for Monica Dickens to the Prince of Wales investiture for the Queen. By a technique of her own invention, Mrs Stancombe paints free-hand on silk and chiffon: Concorde's pilot wore her specially designed badge on the first trip to France. Mrs Stancombe's house perpetuates the name of Ironside, the son of Ethelred the Unready, who led the Battle of Sherston in 1016.

The hero of the battle, which took place on the Cliff, was a local man, John Rattlebone. Local heroes, like old soldiers, never really die, generations of Sherstonians must have passed on these lines like a kind of creed for they were still being recited in the year 1657—six and a half centuries after Ironside's men sent Canute's soldiers packing:

Fight well, Rattlebone
Thou shalt have Sherston
What shall I with Sherston doe?
Without I have all belongs thereto?
Thou shalt have Wyck and Willesly
Easton Towne and Pinkeney.

It is the ancestral home of fighting men, in the churchyard is the memorial of George Strong, one of the first soldiers to be awarded the V.C., no mean achievement in the Crimean War for a lad of nineteen.

Already a strategically-placed camp before the Romans came; the early Britons no doubt welcomed the military strength the invaders poured into their fortifications which earned Sherston the name of the City of White Walls. Records speak of it as a large city and an important military outpost stretching almost into Tetbury. The Saxons named it on account of its *scyr* 'white, shining' stones and The White Town is mentioned several times in the stirring poem by Llywarch Hen.

By the time the Normans sought it out it had a church, of which only the effigy of Rattlebone remains, and was privileged to hold markets and fairs. The Tolstoy marks the site of the old market, the base of the market cross being planted in the new vicarage garden.

History raises its hoary head everywhere in Sherston but it lives happily with its ghosts: it is a bright, bustling village which has pride in its past but makes no attempt to cash in on it.

The Old Royal Ship Inn at Luckington and white gulls following the wake of a tractor seem to be directing the Fosse Way to its destination.

Alderton still keeps faith with the Cotswolds with its church roof. One of its fonts dates from Saxon times and we may be gratified to read in the ancient records that Bishop Hooper in his examination of the clergy in 1551 found Alderton's rector well learned and "able to preach". But as we return to the Roman road at Littleton Drew we find it has left the Cotswolds completely.

The Fosse Way has attracted but a handful of villages as it marches like a resolute legionary north-east from its great Cotswold capital by way of Lewis Lane to Hares Bush and Ragged Hedge Covert, crossing Ampney Downs to where the modern A429 carries fast-moving traffic along its straight course. The Romans still punctuate its passage—Hollow Foss, Fosse Cross and Fosse Bridge, and remnants of their civilization paraphrased in a ten-mile radius—Yanworth Wood, Listercombe Bottom, Combend, Compton Grove, Withington, Whittington, Barnsley and Bibury, are nowhere better illustrated than at Chedworth Roman Villa.

The Yanworth–Withington turn off the Fosse Way is a rewarding diversion in itself. Here, set at the head of a lovely wooded valley where the custodian's white and black house, originally a shooting lodge, provides an attractive pointer amid dark firs is interpreted the kind of place Virgil wrote of, the home every Roman dreamed of. But for a gamekeeper digging for a lost ferret and finding bits of tesserae it would still be under the Cotswold earth. Now the property of the National Trust, it is the most completely exposed villa in the west of England. The mosaic floors are the *pièce de résistance* made from mostly local materials, the oolite limestone providing the white cubes. Many a homesick Roman gazing idly at the seasons depicted on the floor must have longed for that of Cupid carrying a garland to come, especially when an easterly gale blew mercilessly through the valley.

The museum is stocked with the debris of his life. The rubbish pit has been sifted for bones of the animals and birds he ate, fragments of pottery, bone tools and pins and picks, stone figures of his household god, even the shears with which he trimmed his beard (as well as shearing his sheep); the earth has yielded all. Even our mod-con bred society find the Roman's obsession for bathing worthy of study. That it was an elaborate process and an architectural feature is well-defined in the existing plan. That the spring which supplied the villa with its watery needs was dedicated to the water-goddess has been revealed by the *Nymphaeum* close to a track leading off to the White Way. That the nymph wields her powers less for the English visitor than she did for her Roman master was evidenced by a little note at the end of last summer's extra dry season: the spring supplying the toilets had dried up—the nearest public conveniences would be found at North-leach! One wonders if Censorimus would have hurtled up the valley and three miles along the Fosse to the nearest town!

Travellers in less haste leave the villa wrapped in the evocative spicy scents of shrubs and yew and many a backward glance of where Horace could have meant by his dream of "a little bit of land with a garden; near the house, a spring of living water, and beside it a small wood".

Woods, in fact, are the prominent feature hereabouts. Stowell Park has its own foresters as befits an estate of its size and standing. I recall a late autumn afternoon and asking three young men at the sawmills about their work, for here in the valley were craftsmen who were making gates and hurdles and all manner of wooden things for implements in the centuries-old way from larch, oak and spruce for maintenance of the estate. Apart from their work not receiving the acclamation it would had they become members of a craft guild, was the fact that these young men thought it "wouldn't look right" if they had their photo taken grouped around the fire—the only bit of light left—my watch said it was past their knocking off time, a curl of smoke from Sawmill Cottage signalled tea-time in the Davies's household, but these conscientious workers (whom everyone declares are a lost tribe) were not prepared to leave until "all was safe and tidied up". Unfortunately, the smoky bonfire did not provide sufficient light for my camera's eye—the photo was not clear, but the impression they made on me was.

Farmington coppices also have their woodmen. Ash poles, some for turnery others for broomhandles, with a small amount of beech and oak for furniture are being replaced by spruce and larch. Again, the estate has a call for its own supply of hardwoods.

The Cotswold village of Farmington can bear little resemblance to its namesake in North America which has a population 150 times larger. It is tempting to follow the fortunes of the other twin, especially when the rector from the New World comes to Old Farmington and brings with him snippets to delight either. One such story was when Mark Twain on being presented to Queen Victoria was asked from where he came. When he said Hartford the Queen was no wiser until he explained that "to the west of it was Farmington".

To mark the three-hundredth year of Connecticut's founding, Farmington had the village pump roofed for its Cotswold cousins: a bird-bath stands outside a library in Farmington, U.S.A., quarried from the Cotswold oolite at the quarry, formerly known as the Fosse Quarry, which is still worked beside the Roman road.

A quartet of villages just north of the Fosse Way makes another pleasant diversion. Hampnett seems almost an outpost since the

Bibury—with Arlington Mill across the bridge

Mike Hart's study of the Leach enigma is eagerly awaited. Here (*above*) the river has made one of its brief winter appearances in the deeply cut valley near Sheepbridge, Eastleach. (*below*) The charming Coln from Coln St Aldwyn Hill

(*above*) Patricia Haines spinning on the wheel made by her husband based on the design of the original cottage spinning wheel. (*below*) Theo Merrett, leatherworker of Far Oakridge

Tump Cottage at Barrow, near Cheltenham, David White's first contract for thatching on his own. The cottage is of fifteenth-century origins; traces of a monastery floor were discovered three feet below the lawn

old road was diverted, a quieter place than when the coaches rumbled through it. One remembers Turkdean for its glorious avenue of beech trees drawing the road up from the moss-lined bowl in which Lower Dean nestles.

Notgrove takes its name, according to an old poem: "From Nut tree groves which border on ye same". The nut trees seem not so prolific today in the hedgerows where the quick-growing thorn dominates, but are kept ever-green in the tapestry worked by the villagers themselves. It is a charming chronicle of the village, designed by Colin Anderson of Notgrove Manor to raise funds for church repairs. What a labour of love it represents. Initials of the principal workers between the angels, emblems and witticisms, symbols and epigrams make it local and lively. During the eleven years while it was being worked the Manor suffered a fire; a phoenix has been appropriately included.

The church is thought to be the site of a Roman burial ground. The Saxons left it a crudely carved stone crucifix, the Norman church builders hastened to the spot and left a bit of their work, the decorators decorated it and the scrapers scraped it. Medieval friars sleep in stone and even Dick Whittington's uncle chose this little spot to rest.

This is farming country. No hedge or wall separates field from field so that at harvest-time it seems that one goes through the golden corn to Alyworth where a string across the road halts the odd car to allow dairy cows passage to their parlour at the bottom. A very wise precaution safeguarding both car and cattle.

Aston Blank is now no more. By the nod of a committee, the centuries old burden of bearing two names has been lifted from the tiny village which will, henceforth, be known officially as Cold Aston. Originally plain Aston, it became 'Cold' in 1255, then 'Blank' in 1535. The Post Office used the former, the Ordnance Survey the latter and signposts bore both.

The minor road leading to Bourton-on-the-Water rejoins the Fosse Way close to the Roman settlement. Stow-on-the-Wold is the horse fair town of the Cotswolds and echoes of its former self can be heard in the secret language spoken by dealer and buyer when the colour and cadence of the Cotsall and Romany tongues rise and fall over the bargains.

Broadwell clusters around its green, a neat village with a good style about its houses and barns and so to Donnington through a

H

shallow ford. New houses blend well with the older ones and a fine honey-coloured wall wears its newness with pride. Again, the *agger* asserts itself. The road marks the main street of Moreton-in-Marsh, the last Cotswold town on its route. As we reach Dorn, a ghost-like cluster of old cottages amidst cabbages and corn, the countryside flattens, ferns and nut-bushes replace stone walls and the one stone-tiled roof was so matted with dead ivy and moss that I knew the Cotsall slatter was a foreigner to this former Roman settlement.

7

The Roman Streets

ERMINE STREET: CIRENCESTER TO
WITCOMBE
AKEMAN STREET: CIRENCESTER TO ASTHALL

> There was a young lady from Ciceter
> Who went to consult a solicitor
> When asked for her fee
> She said, "Oh, diddley dee,
> I only came here as a visitor".

A s we have made Cirencester the pivotal spot from which to follow
the Roman roads, it may not come amiss to mention the variations
on its name which may confuse non-Cotsallers. This little ditty
illustrates the pronunciation which was always regarded as 'county',
but in actual fact was in use when folks wrote as they spoke as
testified by an inscription in the church. Four syllables did not have
the lyrical quality for Shakespeare's pen, so we find "our town of
Cicester" in *Richard II*. The worst of all is 'Siren', for what is
wrong with the full-bodied Cirencester as recorded in the *Anglo-
Saxon Chronicle*?

Ermine Street is a splendid illustration of the Roman's ability to
build a road in uncompromising directness between two points—
Corinium and *Glevum*, today's Cirencester and Gloucester. But the
seeker-out of villages must once more deviate from the Roman road
for it passes through none along its sixteen miles.

Bagendon is known to every archaeologist. Being on a tributary
it probably belongs to the Churn valley rather than 'just off the
Roman road', but its chapter is a preface to Caesar's story and can

be read from the fragments preserved in the Corinium Museum. The ancient town of *Caer-Cori* had lain for centuries beneath the soil and but for the resolute scholar Mrs Elsie Clifford, would still be there.

The weird and woaded wildmen, Caesar would have us believe the Dobuni to be, emerge in a different light when excavations reveal intrinsic proof of their civilization; primitive compared to the Roman's, but still a far cry from an animal existence.

The village nestles cosily into an unspoiled valley. The Saxons built its lovely stone church when they went fearlessly through the old Britons' defence dykes, and paid little heed to the flood level of the brook. The floor of the nave was raised two feet in 1832 to combat severe flooding but proving an ineffective measure it was restored to its original level fifty years later. The church as usual is a veritable store-house of ancient treasures, not least of which is a pair of stirrup-topped bell clappers from the Middle Ages.

Bagendon still wears its farming air with its fine barns, a mill with machinery *in situ*, and sounds of rooks and cows and pigeons and farm carts.

A ramble along the valley takes one into the realms of history preserved in field names: Merchants' Downs and Halfpenny Hill.

Back on Ermine Street the 'Five Mile House' and 'The Highwayman' make welcome stopping places. At the pace the ubiquitous Cobbett journeyed one could perhaps understand, if not actually appreciate, that this long stretch on the high road between two valleys presented a cheerless picture. He rated the turnip crop poor and the whole idea of dry stone walls ugly. Altogether, he heaped disparaging adjectives on our stones so a village like Elkstone just to the east would be lost on him, for its very name springs from the stone of which it is built.

Visitors are stray people at any time in Elkstone, in the wintertime they must be lost folk for it is a lonely upland village. Its church is the highest on the Cotswolds at 900 feet and we realize why the tower walls are almost four feet thick. Idiotic behaviour in the past has barred the casual visit to the columbarium over the chancel. No doubt the serious student would receive the necessary permission to climb the newel stairway and see for himself this rare feature.

In an area so rich in Saxon and Norman work—no fewer than

thirty being encompassed in this ten mile square—it would take a brave man to proclaim one of more interest than another, but eminent antiquaries are agreed that Elkstone is chief. The feature that weighted this decision must be the Norman tympanum over the south door, adjudged to be one of the most notable in the country.

One couple who wrestled with the elements on this lonely spot are Mr and Mrs Crewe, whose philosophic acceptance of life in general and isolation by winter snows in particular must have sent many a motorist on his way with many a second thought after he had been 'filled up' from their hand-worked petrol pump.

Winstone on the west of Ermine Street is another bleak spot to which few visitors are attracted, yet the villagers seem to stay and even introduced non-conformity to it.

It is worth searching for Syde and here again is the kind of barn which delights the heart of every true Cotsaller, the buttressed stone walls look strong enough to withstand a siege. Traceried medieval windows wink in the sunlight inviting a second look; perhaps it once served a more ecclesiastical purpose situated as it is close to the Norman church. All is not old though: a stained glass window has been recently dedicated to the memory of Simon Virgo, one-time reporter on our local paper whose later connections with international publishing are illustrated by an open Bible.

Brimpsfield's beauty is in its position by an ever-climbing sinuous road leading up through Caudle Green; its glory is in its past—a flick back through history takes us to the Norman lords whose descendant John Giffard figured so largely in the rebellion against Edward II. Giffard attacked and plundered the royal baggage train on Ermine Street as Edward was pushing westwards against the lords of the Welsh Marches. Giffard's castle was demolished and he was later hanged outside Gloucester city walls. Trees cover the moat, and earth the foundations, but there is no difficulty in finding the site close to the churchyard and noticing how its stones have been well utilized throughout the village. An earlier castle, built by the Normans, was closer to the Roman road.

Birdlip has been bedevilled by the traffic of all ages. There can be few people who have never heard of Birdlip—its name crops up in road warning broadcasts, a place to be avoided in adverse conditions. Wheezing lorries and fogs and frosts and deep snow-drifts cling to the tortuous plunging road which in spring and

summer and autumn affords such an enchanting drop down into
Gloucester.

It is an obvious spot for the old turnpikes, the 'Catchbars' being
the bane of a drover's life. But memories are as long as a man's native
wit and the ancient track which followed the Cotswold Ridgeway
was brought into use on the far side of the bars. The path is partly
a field track and in parts a green lane which follows through to
Buckle Wood Common. No cattle rests at Birdlip any longer, the
great markets are a dim memory; today's beasts hurtle past in heavy
lorries augmenting the traffic flow. In fact, to most travellers Birdlip
means the Hill.

The seventeenth century brought it a new coach road through
the steep woods of Witcombe Park and the Black Horse Inn must
have been a welcome break at the top for both horse and driver.

The village itself is small and one is surprised to find its Cotswold
church counts its age in decades and not centuries, a former one—
described as 'poor'—was burnt down. The east window is the work
of Edward Payne, the Cotswold stained-glass artist.

Hill villages generally keep a closer alliance with tradition than
those of the valleys. May Day at Birdlip Primary School means a
May Queen and a decorated school with Pop Goes the Weasel, the
Cuckoo Dance, Tom Pate and Cumberland Weaving danced round
the maypole.

At the foot of the escarpment the ghosts of Ermine Street appear
in flesh and blood. The festivals which draw thousands to the tiny
village of Witcombe leave nothing to the imagination. Fired by the
enthusiasm of the rector the Rev. John Thornton, historians and
librarians and helpers, each panorama of history unfolds in ever-
increasing splendour. An Iron-Age fort entrance, a skirmish by the
Sealed Knot, sheep roasts, pilgrims, drovers and Romans and
Secondary Modern school-parties all have their part to play when
Witcombe presents its past to public view. More than one motorist
speeding along the old Roman road raised his foot and eyebrows as
very authentic legionaries marched steadfastly along to do their
bit at other village fêtes. But there are also the 'real' ghosts of
Caesar's guards to keep perpetual vigil over Ermine Street as it
leaves the Cotswolds.

Akeman Street is the most deserted of the Roman roads radiating from Cirencester. Originally the name applied to the road

which connected Bath (called Akeman-chester by the Anglo-Saxons) to the Midlands north of Oxford, it is thought to have been an early Roman frontier road. It would seem that the Fosse Way superseded the south-western route when the zealous road-builders took it northwards over the ancient Jurassic Way leading to the Humber. To follow the entire length of Akeman Street today is impossible by car, much of it being lost in meadows and obscurity and conformities to the Enclosure awards, but here and there we can pick up its course as we look at the villages east of Cirencester.

Branching from the Fosse Way at Hare Bushes Lodge, Akeman Street can be followed by a minor road crossing Ampney Ridings to Ready Token, where Roman coins are constantly being dug up—a shield boss found where the road cuts across the old Welsh Way is preserved in Gloucester Museum. The straightness of the road is immediately apparent as it leads towards Quenington, but the village, like Coln St Aldwyns, belongs to the river valley so we shall find them in that context later. The Street crosses the Coln just above Coneygar Wood to wander secretly in the cover of William-strip Park. Raising its head for a couple of miles between Hatherop and Eastleach where The Folly woodland chequers it with quivering shadows, pheasants, partridges and pigs are likely to be the only travellers one meets.

No doubt the Romans took full advantage of the site on which one of Cotswold's noblest barns is built. Commanding extensive views along the Leach Valley and within signalling distance of other military camps in the area, it is not surprising to learn that the pillars supporting a long sweep of former cow-bays are purported to be of Roman origin.

Sheepbridge Hill Barn was built in the heyday of domestic architecture when the gentry had taken over completely from the land-owning monasteries. Great estates embraced whole villages and reshaped the face of the countryside, bringing congruity to the area. That little race, the 'estate workers', did much to further this idea. They were local men, or came to settle in the estate cottages, they built with the native stone in a style which showed deference to the demands of Cotswold where church, cottage, manor house and barn conformed to a basic principle. Size and siting being the chief factors distinguishing one from the other. How easily one can become the other is nowhere better illustrated than here, a transition which has been achieved by a trinity of Cotsallers who under-stand the primal concept of Cotswold. The design of Michael S. Wright, the architect, interpreted so skilfully by Alan Churchill, testifies to what so many have strived to analogize as the distinc-tive features of Cotswold: a craftsman's feeling for stone, an artist's eye for detail, a true sense of proportion, the perfect attune-ment between depth and breadth, void and solid: an acquiescence with nature—home to Mr and Mrs Guy Holland, charmingly Cots-wold.

Akeman Street is still a definable track below the wood as it crosses the Leach valley to be traced again east of Sheephouse. It is well worth seeking out Filkins from this point for the student of Cotswold architecture could find no better illustration than this village of stone. And if he is lucky enough to meet George Swin-ford he will learn more from this craftsman than any treatise on the quarrying, making and shaping of our Cotswold stone, for his knowledge is encyclopaedic, his enthusiasm boundless.

At an age when most men doze away quiet afternoons I found this quite remarkable octogenarian at work in a tiny derelict cot-tage translating a block of stone into a bee skep. His hands, I noticed were like my Pop's, gloved by a million cracks from hand-ling stone, the pencil with which he drew the design on the chimney breast was again familiar—short, stubby and blunt. The sunlight filtered through the stone-dust which wrapped the banker, tools, cobwebs and walls in a film of timelessness. Hundreds of hieroglyphics decorated the lime-washed walls, the secret language of the stone-mason recording work past, present and future.

"Man, wife and four children lived here," he said as he led the way upstairs to what amounted to a small bedroom divided by a thin wooden partition.

"How?" was all I could think of as I tried to envisage beds and furniture where onions were laid out to harvest.

"They didn't take up much room for the stairs—just took them up round the chimney breast, no quoins, all built from the stones straight off the land," he said, making short work of the winding rickety stairs down which I was gingerly picking my way. To ask how six people could have got into that one and a quarter up and one down, let alone cook, eat, work and sleep, seemed puerile.

Born in Jubilee year, George Swinford's childhood, like so many children of that generation, was a state to be got over as quickly as possible. His own incredible memory, extended by retaining stories collected by older men, stretches back to bull-baiting, cow-pox vaccinations, pest-houses and workhouses and the Industrial Revolution. He remembers his father starting off from Filkins as the bells rang out for evensong, walking by way of the footpaths all through the night to Tetbury so that he could start at 6 am on the Monday and so get a full week's work in on the church. He can name the last man to be whipped in the stocks—old Fielding—for whom posthumous pity will surely be aroused when the strength of Filkins' great miller, who wielded the whip, is illustrated by his ability to carry two sacks of wheat round a market place.

Mr Swinford's history of Filkins, which I hope will be published sometime, would interest many a student of sociology. His skill not only as a stone-carver but as a wood-carver would have excited William Morris and Gimson. I sat in his carved oak armchair, and marvelled at the skill and patience which had taken two years of 'spare time' to fashion this lovely thing from what had been a beam at Lechlade wharf.

"When I started work at 12," he said, "it wasn't how long will it be, but how *good* will it be?" He showed me a photograph of the oak bedstead he had made for Lady Cripps. The family's coat-of-arms, interspersed with oak trees so reminiscent of Gimson's work, were carved in four panels on each end.

The hand of George Swinford is everywhere in Filkins: his stone carvings of a shepherd, a stone-mason and an albatross on new houses are very like the decorative detail on one of the cottages built as a memorial to William Morris at nearby Kelmscott.

The folk museum, entirely due to Mr Swinford's enterprise, is a chronicle of village life. His personal knowledge of each item magnifies its interest, his interpretation of its history leavened by good Cotsall philosophic humour. It is not a miscellany of old things. There is the 'cadger's' pipe which holds a whole ounce of tobacco. When his father bought it the whole pub smoked it and it took half a pint of beer to put it out. There is his old boneshaker and hand-made nails, a leather bucket from Lechlade's Fire Brigade, a barley ailer and a flail still with its eel skin. "Good boot laces were made with eel skin—feel that, still as tough as leather." There are clay pipes which he found when working the Filkins quarry—

dropped by French prisoners of war after Waterloo, agricultural and blacksmith's tools, steel quoits, window fittings and door locks, a whole range of domestic utensils such as Mrs Beeton would have known, a massive barn lock of 1600—"they had to be big because corn was precious and people so poor". Even the round horseshoes used by highwaymen are there—"they were made round so that it was impossible to know if the horse was coming or going". And for good measure, Mr Swinford has the village lock-up right next door—complete with a mantrap and handcuffs.

The roof of the cell is a single stone slate such as Dr Plot wrote of in his *Natural History of Oxfordshire*, "they dig a sort of flat-stone naturally such, without the help of Winter and so strangely great, that sometimes they have them seven foot long and five foot over . . . and I have seen a small Hovel, that for its whole covering has required no more than one of these stones." These great stones still edge the village today.

Filkins still has its working forge, Mr Trinder no longer shoes horses, a craft which cost him an eye, his skill with iron has turned to more creative work to bring him and his son orders from all over the country.

Craftsmen are the pride of Filkins, where in the village centre, built at the expense of Sir Stafford Cripps, to whom the village also owes its stone-built council houses and cottages for old people, a plaque accords due credit to the work carried out under George Swinford's foremanship: "this building has been erected by crafts-men of the Cotswolds to commemorate the labour of their count-less fellow workers which has enriched the beauty of our country-side in the earnest hope that the people of the Cotswolds will be strong in their determination to preserve that beauty".

This is an area of stone quarries (and wells) Westwell, Holwell and Broadwell were famous for good slates, put to local use as can still be seen and transported to roof many of Oxford's fine build-ings.

A great monolith, with a brass numeral from Ypres cloth hall's clock, makes a striking war memorial in the tiny village of West-well where time seems to be suspended over the duck pond: an illusion heightened one summer morning when the only sound was the chink of metal against stone as a man scraped lichen off his roof.

Remembering that stone 'slats' were known to the Romans,

we return to Akeman Street as it asserts itself as a road once again alongside Broadwell (pronounced Braddle) Grove.

Beyond tall grass and rusty-topped sorrel, Army huts on the left linger from war-riven days, white-washed and well-equipped they house a special hospital. Behind the screen of trees on the right is the Cotswold Wild Life Park, where a most enterprising venture in the field of education has been centred. Its potential being realized by Mr M. N. Molesworth, who first used it as a research base from Oxford University where he is Staff Tutor of Education Technology ('aids to learning' he prefers to call it), it is now a residential centre in which school parties can explore every aspect of the environment making full use of the park facilities.

I couldn't at first understand how the animals, birds and reptiles captured from the South American and Asian plains could be related to conservation of the wild life of our own environment, but a Sunday morning spent with Mr Molesworth, watching the groups of children working at their projects and reading the material displayed on the classroom walls was answer enough. Starting with the exotic, the children were able to comprehend the difference between the 'foreigners' and the 'natives', and there are plenty of 'locals' to be found in the natural sanctuary—thrushes and finches, owls and badgers, deer and woodcock, pheasants and wagtails, a whole range of British wildlife: careful measurements of the beaks of a toucan and a wren, and why they were so vastly different, illustrated the point.

There seems no limit to the possibilities of the centre—zoology, biology, botany, natural history, ecology, arts, history, geography . . . artists, poets, craftsmen, and even musicians who equated music with the animal and bird sounds, have been able to wring even a wider spectrum out of the already full curriculum—ideally suited to team-teaching.

Secluded from the teeming main Burford–Swindon road by fine oaks, beeches and chestnuts, with the White Horse hills touching the distant skyline, the children of a Solihull school were exploring every possible area as a maths project: cages were measured and animals observed for amount of movement involved; the results carefully charted to see whether particular species really did have sufficient room for its size and nature, nor was it just a novel way of making a monotonous subject less so—the findings are valuable to the curator, Mr Brian Sinfield. All kinds of interesting factors are brought to light. A little group was measuring the rhino enclosure and we discovered, by the sudden interest it showed in the white measuring tape, the rhino's vision to be about twenty yards. In close proximity to Brize Norton R.A.F. base, up-to-the-minute world news can be obtained and should a venturesome finger be poked into a cage labelled 'this animal bites', Burford's cottage hospital is but yards away.

Mr Molesworth, officially appointed—but unpaid—as Director of the Park's Education Department spares neither himself nor his professional knowledge to further this venture. The ultimate aim is yet more demanding—that of building a residential unit for the disabled and handicapped. The project, one of the most ambitious in the country, is past the planning stage. What was missing, of course, was the price tag. The Education Department is a registered charity and a national appeal for funds is afoot.

As he showed me the small matchwood model amid its twig trees I could envisage the unit of lecture and practical rooms, with wheelchairs propelled along to the observation tower, from where wild life could be seen enjoying practical conservation under the sycamores and chestnuts, families enjoying a day out, and school parties working from the textbook nature has written. A commercial enterprise exploited for educational purposes would have pleased the great Socrates.

Shilton's broad ford is a natural haunt for ducks, a friendly colony who will eat everything you offer—except brussels sprouts!

Akeman Street runs through the small village of Asthall. The beautiful gabled Elizabethan manor, childhood home of Nancy Mitford, vies for importance with the church, both situated on rising ground out of the flood level, whereas the Windrush waters would rise to the cottage windows 'and into your waistcoat pockets'—lower in the village before drainage became a common precaution.

The threads of history draw the ages together in a fascinating way, for here, at the easternmost point of the Cotswolds, we find the chapel takes us back to the story of Hailes and the Holy Blood. Lady Joan Cornwell sleeps a stately stony sleep in the north chapel, a silent guard over this spot which was once possessed by Edmund, the King of the Romans' son.

An ancient barrow, the most eminent on Akeman Street, stands like a mile-stone directing the Roman road out of the Cotswolds and on to Alchester. But ghosts linger. 'Old Blue Stockings' lurked in the meadows and a phantom team haunted the road. I like the story of the farmer who, awakened by his wife's agitated whispers that someone was in the house, said, "Put your head under the clothes and let us die like men".

8

The Outer Wolds and Evenlode Valley

EBRINGTON HILL TO IDBURY

EBRINGTON HILL, geologically speaking, terminates the Cotswolds' eastern edge abruptly. But as there have been as many definitions of what is Cotswold as there have been writers to formulate them—that very fact emphasizing that the limits are not subject to rigorous definition—I will leave the discussion over non-existent boundaries to the pedants.

Unlike the dramatic sweep of the escarpment on the west, which is seen from Littledean Hill across the Severn as an impressive and almost continuous skyline from Bath to Meon Hill, the eastern edge runs into the wide, flat open vale of the Stour. Extending southwards beyond Moreton as the Evenlode Valley, the Jurassic limestone cuesta is reduced in scale. The Evenlode Valley, wide and shallow in comparison with the sharply incised valleys of other Cotswold rivers, interrupts the continuity of the dip-slope wolds and the difference in character is immediately apparent. Villages are liberally sprinkled along this outer edge so let their individuality guide us rather than a ridgeway or Roman road.

I like to start at Meon Hill first to savour contrast, for this northern outlier wears the coat of both camps: on the west sleeve are the tangled beech roots and rich red earth of Cotswold warmly wild, on the east a cultivated arm of golden cornfields and tamed earth salutes the morning sun over the vale.

Lush vales. Tiny boys on tiny trikes were herding cows into

Ilmington where I found a hurdle-maker—again, a handsome young man with wife and family to match, following an old craft in the time-honoured way. Willows are plentiful in this area but the ash, preferred by most farmers, is brought from as far afield as Hampshire and Shropshire, and Mr Vincent's hurdles pen not only the sheep of the Cotswolds and the vale but those as far away as Berwick-on-Tweed—an indication of the paucity of hurdle-makers.

Ilmington Downs and Windmill Hill are for fresh spring mornings and hot summer afternoons: grass and earth smell sweet; space and silence swim and sing all around. Cotswold will reveal its secret to its true lovers. For those whose raptures are aroused not by tumpy grass and cuckoo-flowers and tangled briars there are the velvet lawns and camellias and magnolia hedges of nearby Hidcote and Kiftsgate. But there is no rigidity in the way beauty has been cultivated at these two famous gardens. Hidcote has its satellite hamlets and Kiftsgate its hill; both are held close to every horticulturist's heart. Both afford delightful views.

Battle Bridge excites the imagination but records are reticent as to which battle it commemorates. References to the Saxons sending yet another bevy of British chiefs fleeing from 'a field under Kampdene' is one theory put forward to justify its existence.

Ebrington wears the thatched hairstyle and fruit-decked apron of the vale, but its feet are in the Cotswold hills. And they stick their runner beans as we do. Seats on a triangular green perched on one of its many shelves afford a welcome rest for those whose 'legs are older than their teeth'.

Blockley no doubt owes its existence to the brook which bears its name and one can't help thinking the old bishop of Worcester had a bargain when he bought it from King Burgred for 300 shillings 'in silver'. He wouldn't of course, recognize the large village group up on the hillside where his flock of thirteen hundred sheep ambled in thirteenth-century bliss.

One is always surprised to find industry in the Cotswolds, but the extensive ribbon trade of Coventry sent probing fingers to catch what power it could from the hill streams farther south. A silk mill for silk-throwing (making twisted threads ready for weaving in Coventry) opened in Queen Anne's reign. There were six, employing some six hundred people, by the time Victoria was celebrating her Golden Jubilee and the mill workers relied on the church bell toll-

ing at 5 a.m. to rouse them for an early start to their long day. A
new vicar was horrified at this secular use and stopped it, but
acquiesced to public opinion after riots had broken out which took
eight policemen from the surrounding villages to quieten.

Despite these industrial overtones which bred terraced houses
and chapels and left deserted mills to become 'eagerly sought-after
residences', there is a harmony about the place as each building
finds its foothold on the hill shelf or beside the stream. White-
shirted men bob as black woods roll on the village green while
white fantail pigeons gossip cosily on a Cotswold stone dovecote
and dark shadows sleep in the big pond from where electricity was
generated, so affording Blockley church to be the first in the country
to have electric light.

A recent discovery of human bones unearthed from the foundations of the former Bell Inn had the villagers delving deeply into
their memory stores. The churchyard used to extend at one time to
the pub site, a doorstep being formed from an old tombstone. But
the mystery of the bones may be locked in the dark chapters when
prisoners were 'rested' there in transit to Worcester gaol. A stone
in one of the attics was called 'the prisoners' stone'.

Woods and walks follow the stream where Addison's essays
are brought to life. And hereabouts are two lost villages. Beyond
Dovedale is Upton which the Anglo-Saxons built, the Black Death
destroyed and the excavators are endeavouring to record. Middle
Ditchford has even disappeared from the map.

A stately avenue of limes stand to attention as one approaches
Batsford. The church stands on a slope keeping an eye on the Park
drive. It is one of those private-looking places which I can never
take seriously. An elaborate marble coffin lid with grapes and doves
and gold mosaic is the ultimate in funereal furnishings. I couldn't
imagine the Lords Redesdale praising all creatures great and small
from their velvet-curtained and cushioned and screened family
pews, but I could understand why Goodhart-Rendel described it as
"the Holy Hon's Cupboard".

Bourton-on-the-Hill has its Horse and Groom Inn with cheery
red doors to tend you at the top of the steep hill which defeated
the first motor car in 1883. No doubt there was plenty of good-
humoured banter from the folks who lived on the hill as horses
hauled it up past their stone-walled gardens. It elongates the
village giving an illusion of size beyond its actual area, and one is

The Waterley Bottom
Mummers

(*above*) Laurie Lee's childhood home of *Cider with Rosie* in the Slad Valley. (*below*) Farmstead seen from Painswick Beacon

(*above*) Sunset over South Cerney water; (*below*) That other Paradise—near Cranham

Hatherop's tricycling tramp

surprised to find that the population is barely half of what it was 150 years ago.

This is well and truly stone country, the quarrymen had their allotments close to the quarry and houses sprang up around the broken ground, but it is at the foot of the hill that the stone asserts itself in full measure as one of the largest barns in the district. Many a church has lowlier proportions, few have such simple dignity. I imagine that inside the lofty nave deep-voiced whispers whispered excitedly when Sir Thomas Overbury's murder by slow poisoning was brought to light. The victim's nephew, master of Bourton House 'next door', appears to have been a scholarly sleuth and must have had the villagers trembling in delicious horror when his account of the *Campden Wonder* was published for the Perry family, being more local than the master's uncle, who was caught in one of the webs of intrigue and jealousy which festered in every dark corner of James's court, would naturally arouse more interest.

It is the forest rather than the river which gives distinction to the Evenlode Valley. Physically, much of it had disappeared if we think in terms of silent and secret woodlands. A forest having metes and bounds, as opposed to wall-enclosed park, spread far and wide in William's day; Wychwood being one of the four largest in the land. Magic and mystery are hidden in old records and cherished stories, but even now the deep, dark shadows are always there as "old Wychwood dons its robe of green".

Evenlode acknowledges its Cotswold origins rightly enough, its stone walls are kept in good order and no feature obtrudes, even the river is fairly insignificant. It is the pottery which takes its name afield.

Chastleton House dominates its village of stone cottages and small church by its size and situation, and hugs one of those delightful escape stories which has magnified in retrospect into heroic proportions. Out of that romantic period, when Roundhead hunted Cavalier and female cunning—with a goodly dose of laudanum—outwitted desperate and dangerous men, it seems a pity that the heroine had not the name poets love to immortalize —at least I have heard of no ode penned to Mrs Jones.

From the high and lonely Chastleton Camp site where the eye and the heart sees and feels so much, it is comforting to be sheltered by the mile length of beech trees along the main road into Adlestrop.

I

We all remember Adlestrop because Edward Thomas remembered it. The name-board which he saw when his train stopped 'unwontedly' in late June is now in the bus shelter. Jane Austen would have known neither when she visited her uncle at the Rectory, but she would, perhaps, have cause to smile as houses are being 'elevated to cottages' again. The whole village appeared to be in the process of being rebuilt but the oaks and elms of the Park and the forest backcloth change but little.

No train stops now at Adlestrop, the station is private property —happily enough it is an Adlestrop-born man, whose grandfather owned the coal-wharf, who tends the rambling roses on the old iron railings. The stream opposite the rail track attracts much bird-life and I watched the lovely grey-backed wagtails while Mr Sedgley pointed out the flowers and bushes that the poet would have seen. A semi-moss rose, the yew which marked the entrance and many of the shrubs remain with the willow-herb and meadow-sweet, the trees acting as a buffer against the noise of the trains. Nephews of Edward Thomas had made the pilgrimage and so had many uninvited folk, who respect neither private notices or other people's privacy. There was a rumble, a rush of air as the Worcester express ripped past, the ground trembled beneath my feet and I felt suddenly very sad that no one would ever again have that simple pleasure of stopping unwontedly at Adlestrop.

The eastern spur of the Cotswolds holds the charming old town of Charlbury in the corner of Wychwood. A century ago the Forest Fairs, throbbing with sinful splendour, thrilled the majority with human and animal freaks, puritanical parents locked their offspring away from the bucolic frolic and revelry ran its riotous route. Lord Churchill, with his equipage of footmen in red plush breeches, white stockings and cockades, drove through the cheering crowds, nodding and smiling genially at the commonalty. He wore a different complexion the following day when the drunk, the debauchee and the pick-pocket were hauled up before him.

Border villages like the Tews and Churchill, Spelsbury and Enstone speak of both Cotswold and the forest, but lore and legend, fact, fable and fiction lurking in the hoary old stones crouching like so many prehistoric monsters makes a Cotsaller hasten back to the hills, to the cosiness of the dells or the freedom of the wolds, where we know our ghosts and religious rites are those of seed-time and harvest, not solidified in stone circles and strange forest laws.

Two of Daylesford's sons became famous but neither severed their Cotswold roots. Freddie Grisewood expressed affection for his home at every opportunity, as every Cotsaller who listened to his broadcasts knows. Macaulay's pages hold the story of how Warren Hastings dreamed his dream beside the stream and the dream came true. The vicissitudes between the opening and closing chapters of Hastings' life-story are too well known to bear repetition here—perhaps one day when pantomime and fairy-tales have tired of Dick Whittington they will turn to the pages of the British Empire and the golden walls of Daylesford House to find their day-dreaming hero.

The fame and infamy which chequered Hastings' career were followed with keen interest by the locals. Bells rang and wine flowed freely at the news of his acquittal. His memory rests in ivory chairs and golden bedsteads and a big memorial urn. His great-grandfather, on the other hand, was more honoured by the old farming fraternity for he was the *patronus* of sainfoin, that blaze of brilliant pink which was so much part of our landscape and an important fodder for sheep and cattle before turnips became fashionable. It is heartening to know that the certified Cotswold stock seed is still grown at the Manor Farm, Chadlington.

A Daylesford squire nearer our own time poured his wealth into founding the famous Kingham Hill School. That Kingham was held close to local affections was illustrated by an old man saying he would "rather be hanged in Kingham than die a natural death at Churchill". It certainly seems that its inhabitants held sway if the story is true that the man who did not wish to be buried underground was built into the wall of the church instead. Kingham station echoes to the engineering fame of Brunel, but the O.W. and W. (the Old Worse and Worse) took over and the G.W.R. acquired the complete line and few locomotives.

Bledington is on the Gloucestershire side of the Evenlode; the hand of the Cotswold mason is still there in the church to give emphasis to the 'rock of ages', there are tall red-bricked chimneys and low brick buildings from the local brickworks. A new roof of Cotswold stone caught my eye, so I noticed the maypole on the village green.

Monarchs are well presented—Henry VIII keeps a close watch on the patrons of the pub, Victoria's jubilee clock keeps worshippers strictly to time, a bell resting in the chantry lets the "belles of Bledington" speak to the village with their iron tongue, while it reminds "And Charles he is our King 1639" and an old book of prayer illustrates the "Powder Plot of November 5th", giving thanks for the happy deliverance of James I. The hourglass is gone, the bracket remains, but judging from such homely touches as an album of photographs and a box of dolls there was the feeling that here the depth of divinity was no longer measured by length or duration.

Fuzzy, hazy television reception may be but a memory in this area if the ponderous wheels of preservation committees allow the Round Tower of Icomb to be demolished in order that a television tower should be built in its place. I couldn't help thinking that if the embattled Guy's Folly had not been left to face the ravages of the elements across the bleak upland, with never a pat of plaster on its rotund form, the question of its removal may have never arisen. As it is, the winds tumble unchecked through its gaping window frames and race dizzily around its cornerless rooms. It howls like hollow laughter as we pause in the road and remember that inside one could literally boil the kettle in Gloucestershire and drink the tea in Worcestershire—the county boundaries running through the fireplace. Built on the site of an Iron Age camp it commands sweeping views all around, Stow-on-the-Wold appears but a handful of grey stone beyond the cornfields and the Fosse Way but a taut thread. A lady in the village told me that there was a stone in the trees of The Drum earthwork which even a team of horses couldn't budge.

It is easy to understand why Icomb was three times winner of the coveted Bledisloe Cup for the best-kept village. Its green apron is neatly trimmed and great pride is taken in its appearance, reflecting credit on the Icombians—a mere 120 strong, some fifty less than a century ago when the dwindling population and extinct gentry were reckoned the chief cause of the ancient church mouldering away. Then, as now with the tower, someone noticed it crumbling and decided to do something about it. Festooned with flowers, the church was re-opened in great style and the congregation celebrated on the Rectory lawn, doing justice to a "plentiful cold collation".

An old soldier of Agincourt bequeathed his body to Icomb and three shillings and fourpence to the Mother Church of Worcester. His stone effigy reveals no secrets but records whisper of underground passages leading from the church to his manor house and on to Bruern Abbey. With so many vantage points all around from which the eyes of ages could chart a man's every move, it was probably a wise precaution to have human 'oonts' burrowing through the ground.

Yet another underground passage from the abbey tunnelled into Shipton-under-Wychwood to the Shaven Crown Hotel, a fourteenth-century guest house built by the monks. The village takes its name from the 'ship' (sheep) which were the greatest asset of the monastery, and the forest in whose bounds it once stood. A hunting lodge in Queen Elizabeth's day, the hotel retains a medieval splendour in its timbered great hall. The detail on the carved stone archway would have been crisper when she passed beneath it, but time has mellowed it and zealous owners have cared well for it.

Wychwood was well-known to the Tudor queen—Woodstock where she was kept a prisoner not far away. She presented the monk's guest house to the village on condition that it became an inn and a charity to be formed for the needy. John Foxe, author of the *Book of Martyrs*, and William Langdon of the *Vision of Piers Plowman* lived at Shipton.

A stone on the broad green, dated 1851, marks the spring which supplied the village with water before the fountain was erected close by. Ironically, it is a memorial to seventeen parishioners who perished at sea on a voyage to New Zealand in 1874.

What countryman has not found delight in the publication of that name? Having met its founder, Robertson Scott, a white-haired nonagenarian, white-bearded like a prophet, gentle as Jesus and as wise as Solomon when I was in my teens and in awe of anyone who wielded a pen let alone published, I wondered if Idbury claimed to be Cotswold. It is set on one of our hills and the old records say "the true Cotswold men who love to be free" resented the old laws and restrictions of the forest which Charles I tried to revive.

"Oh! glory yes", Mrs Field looked up from her vigorous polishing of the gnarled pews, "if I couldn't get up in the morning to see my hills, oh, dear!" The unlikely prospect obviously filled her with dismay. "These Cotswold buildings will last for ever and ever.

Amen," she added automatically as she looked round the old church.

She told me, between bursts of rubbing polish on and off, of jam-making during the war in the kitchens of the manor with an old friend of mine whom I was going on to visit in hospital.

"Helen! Well, glory be," she exclaimed. "You tell her we're still making jam—not in the manor, of course. That is a finishing school now. That's why these wires are on the ends of the box pews—they're to hold the candles for the Nativity play which the school puts on—we have a real donkey, a real lamb and a real baby. You tell Helen she wouldn't know the place since she was companion to Mr Scott—oh, lovely man he was. The old forge is now a community centre and we sell jams and pickles and pies which we make ourselves. No, she wouldn't know it now, people come from all over for our apple pies—like Piccadilly Circus it was last Saturday. I counted *ten* cars, Yellocks! I nearly forgot to show you."

She tiptoed across the floor and put on the belfry light. "Our only bit of stained glass, isn't it lovely." I agreed it was—a tiny window of ancient glass which could be viewed from the nave.

In the churchyard I found the ornate tomb of Sir Benjamin Baker, the architect who built the old Forth Bridge, and watched the Red Arrows performing their amazing aeronautic acrobatics over a field of uninterested sheep while Wychwood forest lurked like a dark cloud against the skyline. But nothing could equal the humble pride of being allowed to share the pleasure of Idbury's accidentally discovered treasure.

9

The Ways of the Windrush

THE SWELLS TO MINSTER LOVELL

THE tributaries of the Windrush, the Dikler and the Eye, each support pairs of villages. The Swells, Upper and Lower, are linked by the clear Dikler just west of Stow-on-the-Wold. Our village fathers chose their sites well and men through the centuries have watched sunlight glinting on this silvery water. What picture Lower Swell would present today had the chalybeate spring discovered last century been fully exploited, one shudders to think. That an attempt was made to attract the hard-drinking squires to the fashionable spa waters lingers yet in the ornately-façaded Spa Cottage where the oriental influence appears to have seeded from the exotic species at Sezincote. But it only serves to complement what is so Cotswold in the villages, like a piquant spice added to a local dish.

It is to the visible head of the Dikler all Englishmen would make a pilgrimage if the Donnington Brewery threw open its doors to let them sniff their fill. To do so would defeat the object. It is a private family business; one of a handful of independent breweries who own their public houses.

The intricate processes of brewing were explained to me by Mr Arkell, the owner. I ran hops in pellet form through my fingers and climbed up ladders to peer down into huge wooden vats where dark depths heaved delicious smelling sighs from beneath creamy foam. Six hundred gallons are brewed at a time to serve the seventeen Donnington houses within fifteen miles of the brewery. Malted barley is produced at Cirencester. The purity of their own spring water was the deciding factor when the brewery was established in

1863. Originally a woollen mill, which became in turn a cornmill with bakehouse, the buildings form a charming group beside the lake, which has been enlarged from the mill pond, now a water-fowl's paradise. Mr Arkell took me down into the gardens and fed his fish. Rainbow trout flashed into the sunshine then disappeared in a sparkle of droplets. The mill wheel creaked and splashed the marginal plants—colour, shapes, sounds—the cult of simplicity: a grandeur not easily attained.

Another mill wheel churns through the waters of the River Eye before they prink prettily through Lower Slaughter. I like to go when summer trippers have left it to the villagers. Then one sees a cottager in 'wellies' carrying a basket of greens across to his neigh-bour. I have sat for hours watching the reflections of the little grey house with its no cycling badge and shiny brass door knob and the tall brick chimney of the mill settle in the stream—a pied wagtail skating the surface will make the straight chimney tremble and the whole reflected picture shakes and buckles until it looks like a Disney drawing. What a pity 'Wayside' has but two tiny leaded windows so that its people don't look over this delightful corner, a robin whistles a happy tune clearly through the silence, he can see it all from his frosted bramble bush.

Even the council houses are roofed with native stone and happily there are no tourist trappings although it has been compared to Bourton-on-the-Water and certainly appears on most tours of the Cotswold villages.

I go there for the home-made bread. Three generations of Wilkins baked bread at the old mill before the Colletts settled here four-teen years ago. A family of bakers, Martin assured me it was the quality of the water which made the difference to their genera-tions-old recipe which was never so good as it is now at Slaughter. We talked of bread home-made from Gloucestershire flour, and lardy cakes, a Cotswold speciality. I nodded appreciatively while eating one and clucked sympathetically when he said that to make it all possible work started at 2 a.m. The water-wheel still turns. It used to drive the hoist, but stitched flour bags have to be carried, whereas tied bags of yesterday could be hoisted.

Upper Slaughter has none of the tidied-up looks of its sister downstream. It is a delightful place where horseriders are as much a part of its daily scene as motors are to its twin. It, too, has its footbridges and a shallow ford but they were built and used by the villagers and were not meant to form a focal point—so, of course, they do. It is one of the delightful tricks Cotswold plays.

I talked to Mr Broad at Home Farm about his accredited herd of British Friesians and of the difficulties for the farmer individual with the spiralling rents of Cotswold's rich soil. It was late on a Saturday afternoon, young men of his age would be at a football match, a little group of Heythrop hunters, whom I had seen earlier at Wagborough Bush and followed through Naunton, were jogging back home. There were still fifty-six cows to be milked and as many more to be fed before Mr Broad could ease off his heavy wellingtons. Our conversation was carried on during the mucking-out of a satanical-looking bull's stall. I was assured he was "quite a friendly chap" but I didn't put the qualification to the test. There was no rancour in the young man's story of how the village had changed though he seemed a trifle sad that the fêtes, especially that of St Peter's Day, were a thing of the past. The family had suffered the scourge of 1952 when foot-and-mouth disease had wiped out their first pedigree herd. He is a true Cotsaller and knows that a high price is paid for its privileges. Property-seekers measure that price in money, but we know it can draw heavily from the limited golden store of youth.

It is interesting to follow the quarry uplands north from this hill village on the diminutive River Eye and descend the Windrush valley from the river's source just above the lonely village of Cutsdean, whose isolation is due to the peculiarities of monastic ownership going back to Offa's time. It still has the appearance of an island—a huddle of cottages succoured by their own church and pub, stranded amid the rolling plains of Cotswold.

By the time the Windrush has eased itself from its bed and reaches Ford it has already called its choristers together. Birdsong guides it along through the meadows to Temple Guiting but the hill takes the road and fields into the clouds it would seem.

The Knights Templar who had a preceptory at Temple Guiting would have passed under the same church doorway as we do today, but the zealous hand of the restorers has laid heavily and often on the remainder.

Guiting Power is larger. Its houses look over both road and river, which has been supplemented by another small stream hereabouts. All is quiet around its village green and one can chat at the shop with a stable door, but we hear that the good men of

Guiting are prepared to do battle with anyone who tries to interfere with their way of life. Our fore-fathers, so the tell-tale records disclose, were a pretty earth-bound lot when it came to ritualistic innovations in their church. I could imagine the stalwart villagers as they declared emphatically to the local paper that they "did *not* go to church and furthermore *would not*".

A lengthy account followed the arrival of Bishop Hooper's van, which scotched its wheels on the village green. It appears that the vicar and monks, whose monastery door opened to the green, with great magnanimity greeted the missionaries (whose aim was to maintain the Protestant character of the church). The whole village turned out for the meeting, which turned out to be a riotous affair, some of the missiles which were thrown "emitting an odour which to say the least was not savoury", and wordy warfare raged deep into the night.

The school, built by the Waddington family of Guiting Grange, celebrated its centenary in 1972. During which time over two thousand pupils have spent their schooldays. Its 51 primary-age children from the surrounding villages of Naunton, Pinock and Chalk Hill equals the number first admitted.

Naunton is usually viewed from the top Stow road when the red coats of huntsmen are to be seen weaving their way through winter-bared trees in the valley below. Suddenly the structure of Cotswold emerges: old tracks follow the hill ridge and the village nestles close to the river, but when we take a closer look we find its builders avoided the marshy water meadows for it is anchored firmly to the hillside. Happily for the residents no one bothers to go to Naunton except the milkman and errand boys; the postman, of course, can tell you where the local MP lives.

Wyck is the first of the Rissington trio. Gustav Holst had his first professional engagement here; the organ which he played is still in the church. The squire of the day pronounced him "a young man of great promise" and gave him a house on the green where he could study music and give lessons to local people. An elderly lady recalls, "Mr Holst was asked to play at one of our parties, Papa said he was very musical. I don't remember his playing because I was more struck by a tearful little boy—Freddie Grisewood, who lived just over the hill. His father took the services here and Little Rissington."

The village owes much to its rector, the Rev. Harry Cheales, a fact acknowledged by the villagers on his Silver Jubilee. He is a most remarkable man; one may meet him herding a couple of cows through the village, wisps of straw clinging to his clerical clothes, or driving off to some troubled family, juice stains still on his hands from where he had to leave a fine spell of strawberry picking. An erudite authority on things that go bump in the night, the Rev. Cheales has helped many families troubled by poltergeists, his own Rectory with its history of intermittent hauntings, giving him first-hand experience of these restless spirits.

I only wish space allowed me to tell in full the story of how the village was passed over by the foot-and-mouth disease in answer to the Rev. Cheales sending his best cow to a stricken farm in the north. The volition, as with the building of the maze in 1950, was through a vision. The Romans probably sent ambassadors in christianity to our hills for we find most of the old St Lawrence parishes close to their roads. Treading the maze is now traditional on the saint's day. The paths are signposted in the same sequence as the lovely old carvings in the church. Narrow paths fenced with privet and ivy wend beneath the shade of a massive Wellington Pine. One of the first redwoods to be brought to this country, it is now one of the largest with a waistline of thirty-three feet. With a life span of 4,000 years, the tree is an appropriate symbol of eternal life.

The churchyard has another unique tree, a yew some nine feet high has been shaped into a 'living cross'. The wide sweep of the church roof, Cotswold stone-tiles as closely interlocked as the feathers on a bird's wing, is pleasing. A gipsy's grave is marked by a stone near the porch. In true romany fashion his caravan and possessions were burned on top of the hill behind the church on the evening of his funeral.

I thought history was no longer written on tombstones, but a remarkable memorial has recently been raised to a farmer's grave. The carving of a ploughed field with a single furrow plough in front of a dry-stone wall is more poignant than the skulls and crossed bones from the civil war's grim period or the chubby-cheeked cherubs who make death seem such a healthy state. There is much of historic and artistic merit in the church, an exquisitely carved piece of ivory, olive wood plaques and ancient glass showing the total eclipse of the sun in A.D. 1322, even Jesser Ireland's crudely carved message that he "madeth it" are carefully preserved. I retain the present tense despite having just learnt of the theft of the eighteenth-century ivory carving, priceless in that it is carved from a solid piece of ivory so large that it must have been made from a frozen mammoth's tusk, for I have great faith in the spiritual power of Rev. Cheales, who has appealed for the thief to return it unobtrusively to the church where it belongs, after a note inside the offertory box had prompted another erstwhile thief to put in a pound note rather than take the offerings out.

I like to take to the footpaths that link the Rissingtons, and come to Little Rissington alongside where the village must once have stood. As at Oddington, the present village is detached from the church. The records speak of one rector being here sixty years, so he must have lived right through the plague and seen Little Rissington disintegrate. Like Pompeii, the buildings probably fell on the bodies, superstition and contagion would prevent rebuilding on the same site, consequently only the church remains on the north side of the brook. Nature is a great reclaimer. The undulations could be a natural feature of our hillsides, but no doubt itchy spades will not resist forever the temptation to unearth the plan of the former village.

Tradition has been revived again by the Rev. Harry Cheales who is rector here also. His interest in children's singing games has ensured that the Little Rissington version of *The Wind Blows High* will not be lost to posterity. St Peter's Day sees a knot of village children performing the ancient game in front of the church. A couple of shy, blushing youngsters are pushed gleefully into the centre by their friends who dance round them in a circle, their thin voices wavering in the great outdoor space while their feet drum hollowly on the grass.

> The wind, the wind, the wind blows high,
> The rain comes scattering down the sky.
>
> Jane is handsome, she is pretty,
> She is the girl from Rissington city,
> She goes a-courting, one, two, three!
> Please to tell me, who is he?
>
> Kenny Smith says he loves her,
> All the boys are wild about her!
> Let the world say what they will,
> Kenny Smith loves her still.

He takes her down the garden, sits her on his knee
Says My ducky darling, what'll we have for tea.
A china cup and saucer, a guinea golden ring,
A plate to put the porridge on, ding, dong, ding.

The names are changed until everyone has been sung about and danced around.

It is a tradition believed to go back to the Restoration. Another village custom is enforced when courting days lead to wedding bells. The churchyard gate is tied and the bride is lifted over by her groom.

Like Wyck's, the churchyard is beautifully kept and the children place flowers on the graves of young R.A.F. men killed in service at the Central Flying School nearby.

The rolling cornfields of the uplands above the village have given way to the runways and hangars of the airfield. Every year tens of thousands attend the Open Day and thrill to the precision flying of the world-famous Red Arrows and the immortal Spitfires. The station raises vast sums of money for the service's benevolent fund and local charities.

At Great Rissington you climb uphill to the village green and pub and run downhill to the manor, rectory and church. How very parental the Rissington churches are: here, the Great War soldiers are not mere names on board or stone, their faces look bravely at you from a framed collection of photographs.

The river, meanwhile, has chuckled along quite happily in solitude since it was spruced up for Bourton. The Dikler has tumbled into it since then but we see nothing of it again until we reach the Barringtons unless we follow a lane down to cross it over the New Bridge, from where it winds up again through the willows to Clapton-on-the-Hill and the smallest church of the Cotswolds. The churchyard gate is made from horseshoes by a local craftsman, Mr Raymond Phillips. Formerly known as Clapton super Montibus, Rudder found it unworthy of the attention of naturalist or antiquary. I obviously attach much more importance to such simple things as the promise of indulgence for the devout and the strawberry field on the hill summit.

From the tumulus by Bourton Hill farm, Bourton-on-the-Water in the low vale below appears against the blue-green wolds like its own model village. On the west bank, Sherborne's brook hurries along to augment Cotswold's largest river, and provides a mirror in which the village can reflect its beauty. It is a case study for those whose interest lies in examining the structure of a village, the anatomy of Sherborne being severed in two by Sherborne Park. Monastic influences are heavily overshadowed by manorial ones. I would like to have known the early church into whose Norman doorway the postman pops the letters for No. 88. St Mary's joined by a corridor to Sherborne House, is an awesome place peopled with the ghosts of the Duttons. A buxom marble angel crushes a skinny skeleton with her foot, but the skull only leers back at her. One could spend a good hour here studying the craft of the lapicide, and unscrambling the ramifications of Sir John's family.

The mansion came from the mines in the park, which remained open for estate use until the first world war. A quick look round the stone-walled village will show what quantities were used. The stone, like that of Windrush, is white. This 'white happy' element from the Celtic *gwyn* coupled with the *riasc* (morass) became *Windrush*. Windrush stone was used in St George's Chapel, Windsor, and many of Oxford's noted buildings. Mr George Swinford, of Filkins, recalls the extensive mines tunnelling under the Cheltenham road where donkeys were kept in underground stables rather like the pit ponies of the Welsh coal mines. Local stone has been put to good use in building the village which stands well above the water level. The evil-looking beak-heads arched over the church doorway, symbolic of demons waiting to snatch the souls of those attending in an irreverent or thoughtless spirit, seem to have had little effect on the early incumbents for Windrush vicars in general seem to have kept the local gossip-mongers busy. What a-clucking and a-clacking there must have been as one vicar carried a bundle of faggots three times round the cross at Burford as penance for keeping a concubine. Villagers obviously waited not for divine retribution! And it would have paid the Rev. John Drury to remember that one can't be hung for thinking instead of bemoaning the waste of his eighteen pence on a pilgrimage to Hailes. One wonders how much the servant got out of it when he got his master indicted for heresy for declaring the sacred Blood "a fabrication of men's hands".

Now to resort to the Fox Inn and catch up on what's making news today. Here by the log fire one can drink the ale I saw brewed and bottled upstream, and meet the folks of the Barringtons, Windrush, Sherborne and Taynton, the 'Fox' being the only pub hereabouts. Rustler, the friendly boxer, rests his big jowl on the counter—he's heard it all before: cricket scores, how the beans 'turned in', and those 'dalled' townsfolk who snap up the cottages for weekends and think of the farmers as some kind of park-keepers. Then a lady 'with bones' comes in and Rustler gets interested.

The two Barringtons are separated initially by the Windrush and qualification of size: 'Little' sits along a convex edge around a hollow from where the stones for its 'much sought-after' cottages were quarried. A little stream watered it, grass and water-plants grew over the rough depression and a prettier village green would be hard to find.

The 'Fox' lies in a dip beside the river. Dark yews and high park walls draw the road steeply up to Great Barrington.

This is a street village of the great estate, with a well-stocked shop lying 'at the back of beyond' so that 'you have to know where 'tis to know it's there'.

Three generations of the Hall family have worked the smithy's forge. An iron cattle ring on the outside wall spoke of impatient hooves marking time while red hot iron got beaten into shape inside. Today, Bill Hall's hammer beats it into more intricate designs to meet the demand for all kinds of ironwork. While he creates Tudor roses and leaves and squiggles and swirls his son Brian welds some agricultural implement. As the sparks flew from hammer and machine Brian commented on how appropriate Yorkshire's 'Mousey' Thompson's symbol would be in this cell of industry in quiet Barrington.

But the village has had its noisy moments as testified by the tell-tale records. It would seem that the Brays, whose virtues are extolled in no mean manner on their ornate memorials, were not very fortunate in their choice of friends. Thomas Lord Wharton with his brother Harry appear in very bad light when they came to stay and "committed horrible acts in the church of which their servants were ashamed", then went on to "commit disorders" in the village.

The Windrush valley used to ring to the sound of iron upon stone. Here is quarry country *par excellence* which culminates in Taynton. Domesday Book mentions the famous Taynton Quarries but there is a strong belief that quarrymen ground a dusty track to them for a thousand years before.

What an epic tale these rabbit-ridden humps and holes beneath the tufty grass and tangled thorns could tell. And who better could I have to translate these 'hills and hollows' in terms of Oxford's 'dreaming spires', medieval churches, university halls of learning and the princely palace at Blenheim, than Mr Philip Lee whose study of the quarries which he owns and works is extensive, enthusiastic and erudite. A true scholar of Cotswold stone.

Dr Plot in his *Natural History of Oxfordshire* records seeing a waggon load of Taynton stone needing twenty-one horses to draw it. Creaking carts pulled by lumbering oxen must have been a common sight when stone was sent down the Thames from Radcot, near Lechlade. Sir Christopher Wren knew the quarries and chose a local man as his master mason when he set about rebuilding St Paul's after the great fire of London: the fame of the Strongs grew with their buildings. Pittaway is another name which punctuates the records, from the remarkable number of memorials to the family it would seem they lived here for generations, almost all of them quarrymen. Their name is believed to be derived from that very calling.

Taynton itself is one of those small clusters of rural charm which can be taken in at a glance, or, lingering, will keep one occupied for the rest of one's life. Records are musty things unless interpreted in terms of day to day living. I like to think of the tenants planting their three trees each year which the rules of the manor obliged them to do. Some of the ashes, elms and apple trees we see today are no doubt descended from those early steps towards conservation. And why was Edmund Damport allowed to wear his nightcap to church in winter and not his hat? How *old* were the village Methuselahs who are recorded as "ancient batchelour, maide and good householder", and how *poor* were Thomas "the poor fellow, being a stranger; Anne, a poare creature and William Dick, a poor travelling boy"?

Parochial life has played its full role and I can imagine the commotion the "unnaturall murther" of Thomas Fryer caused. What fate befell his son who did the dastardly deed no one knows, but two families suffered the ignominy of having their sons executed at Oxford but a hundred and fifty years ago for a murder of a Forest keeper which they didn't commit.

Mary Countess Talbot of Barrington wouldn't have approved of C. Drew selling his coat which was paid for out of her benefaction, but then the account of how she came by such fortune—her dowry quoted as £80,000, an astronomic sum in those days—would be whispered about by brave men in dark corners for they would have heard down the ages how her father, Adam de Cardonnel, the notorious Secretary of War to John Duke of Marlborough, amassed such wealth.

That local folks could make the punishment fit the crime when it comes to parish politics is illustrated by an instance when a lad of Fulbrook went to claim a Barley Clanger from the Barley Cob Charity. Distributed in Taynton church each St Thomas's Day for poor children of Burford the loaves were, according to the terms of the charity, baked at Barrington from a quarter of barley grown at Sherborne and ground at Windrush Mill. "But," he admitted in his old age, "I 'ad to mek off quick, if they'd a-known I was from Fulbrook and not Burford they'd a-burforded I."

Poachers and highwaymen seemed to have bred pretty thickly around Fulbrook, whose many metal workers gave it the local name of Tinker Town—a handy centre for the illicit hunters' flintlocks. Law on the spot when the blood was hot creates gruesome ghosts from the oft-told tales of Tom, Dick and Harry, sons and terrors of Fulbrook. People still remember being told of how two of the Dunsden brothers hung in gibbet irons at Capps Lodge. It seems that hanging in chains was abolished simply on account of the disorderly rabble which assembled on Sundays to gaze upon them! Local adulation came posthumously: a stone mason used to recut the date and initials each year in the oak tree which formed the Dunsden gibbet.

What a paradoxical picture Death must have presented to a child's eye when the road to church may be shadowed by a limp figure swinging from a tree, swarming with birds and flies, while just down the road at Swinbrook the departed gentry reclined in peaceful magnificence.

> The Traceys, the Lacys and the Fettiplaces
> Own all the woods, the parks and chases

is an ancient chant illustrating the wealth of the old Cotswold families. Disciples of the quaint and curious come by the score to see the Fettiplace effigies. A unique group they make, these six

K

gents of stone still waiting in their tiered bunks as if for the boat-
man of Styx. Fortune and grace is an appropriate motto for this
family favoured by the Tudors, who bought the Manor in 1503.
The family is now extinct but their memory lives on. Miss Peachey
who lives at what was probably the bakery for the vanished
mansion, told me that her father who was a carter had one of the
green coats from the two-centuries-old charity.

"Green is the colour of the Fettiplaces," she explained, "that's
why we have green cloths for Holy Communion. And ifsobe you
wanted a velvet collar on the coat then you paid a shilling."

What a delightful couple the brother and sister Peachey make:
he, a forthright character of country stock, rightly proud of the
boots he'd worn for forty-nine years, his allotment and the biggest
'inons' I had even seen; she in snowy-white apron, her face like a
ripe apple. Griggs drew their like seventy years ago.

I could see, under their direction, the hearts and diamonds
formed of pebbles in the old courtyard where they live and the
marks of carriage wheels. The mansion became tenanted by the
notorious Mr Freeman ('course he wasn't a proper *country* gentleman') a proper Jekyll and Hyde character, wining and dining his
guests at Swinbrook then cutting their throats and pinching their
purses when they were off home on the lonely high roads.

They spoke of the mansion of which nothing remains except
ponds and terraces and snowdrops in the field where Widford's
lonely church beckons the antiquary beyond the grazing white
cattle and clumps of tough rushes, where the trees rustle even on a
still day, to appreciate its Roman villa foundations and be cautioned
by its medieval murals.

The blacksmith who would draw your teeth at his smithy (under
a chestnut tree) with a hand-made key and the shoemaker who
made violins, carving a human face on the fiddle's neck, they have
all gone to the land of once upon a time. But not to this couple
to whom the past telescoped into the present. "Hard luck on that
young bride over at Minster," Mr Peachy said. I agreed, but the
legend of The Mistletoe Bough was ancient in Shakespeare's day!

To the historic village of Minster Lovell the fanatic Feargus
O'Connor took his pipe-dream to make yet another chapter of
Chartist history. A modern housing development now encloses the
Charterville bungalows but they are still recognizable despite
recent innovations of glass-walled porches or a shifted front door.

Only one retains its true originality—even the symbolic rosette over the front porch is kept brightly painted. Mr Bowles whose wife was born there talked to me about the ham rack on the ceiling, the old-fashioned baker's oven and growing corn and potatoes, peas and fruit and a couple of pigs on their original four acres. O'Connor would have been duly gratified. But then he never started with country folk who knew how to resist the temptation of tucking into roast pork when cured ham would fill winter's empty plates. The hungry and unemployed to whom the lottery was directed were city folk who recoiled from tilling the soil and understood not the terms of rural living. Charterville, like its Gloucestershire sister Snigs End, has been pardoned for its presumption and is embraced in the village's ancient arms.

Minster Lovell is old and lovely. But it is to the romantic remains of the old Hall that one is obliged to go. A ghost of its former glory, it stands regal in its ruinous shape, it must have been magnificent in its prime. I will not attempt to embark upon its ancient origins.

One must not miss out the medieval dovecote to appreciate what the old builders could do with rough-hewn knobbly limestone. Disciples of art make pilgrimage to Rome to gaze up to the cloudy concepts of creation—me, I stand in awesome wonder and read what I will from that wooden cobweb, the pegs on which the stone 'slats' are hung pointing the radiating timbers with shadow.

On this memorable stage set by the legend-haunted ruins, the Windrush makes its grand finale as it bows farewell to the Cotswolds and disappears behind the dark curtains of Wychwood.

10

Lively Leach and Clear Coln

NORTHLEACH TO SOUTHROP
CHARLTON ABBOTS TO WHELFORD

THE Leach and Coln both rise, flow and finish completely in the Cotswolds. What the Leach lacks in length it makes up in interest. Its northernmost point is appropriately so named, the infant waters adding some music to the grim ring of Prison Copse, but a feeble source of power when better-watered towns turned their labours to milling cloth. Northleach, as a market-town, will reap its due in other books. What is of interest is that it was created as a market centre where the Cotswolds heavy white fleeces could turn to gold. The hills being almost one large sheepwalk at this time it made sense to set up markets close to main thoroughfares. Close to the Fosse Way mid-way between the markets of Cirencester and Stow was a wise choice and the abbot of Gloucester detached a portion of his manor at Eastington to set up the town in the early thirteenth century.

Northleach has grown and Eastington has dwindled. The famous wool-church of the former with its wealth of brasses attracts visitors from far and wide but I can equally appreciate the skill and artistry which have gone into the kneelers stitched by local women for the humble church at Eastington. Wild flowers in wool gladden the eye and cushion creaking knees. I also recall being shown a most splendid garden tucked behind a cottage in this pocket-sized hamlet where only the Leach bothers to go.

Aldsworth is a sacred spot in our green and pleasant land, for here the pedigree flock of Cotswold breed was saved for posterity by William Garne when the demand for heavy fleeces and large joints went out of fashion.

But these open downs were not always lulled in the pastoral peace we associate with the biblical lamb. Gone are the palmy days of Bibury Races; old maps record the Grandstand and the Jockeys' changing room, but the plough has erased all evidence of their ever being. It is to the archives and stories descended to the older Cotsallers that one has to go to recapture the essence of Nimrod's sporting life.

Bibury Race Club is still very much in existence but at Salisbury, where it has operated all the race meetings held there since 1899. Its peregrinations had taken it from Upton Down where it was founded in 1681 as an outcome of a visit by Charles II to Nell Gwynne at Burford (*cherchez la femme*). State affairs of the Oxford Parliament were no doubt less gloomily anticipated with the Royal Plate to be run for but a ride away. Enclosure of the common fields reshaped the face of the landscape and eased the race-course nearer Aldsworth where, it is recorded, it had no equal in this country. (Why, therefore, it took the name of the next village down the road is a puzzle.)

An ancestor of the Sadlers at Newmarket trained a Derby winner on these downs. One can only marvel at the stamina of 'Dangerous' who took the jockey Chappel safely past the winning post after walking every step of the way from Aldsworth to the Derby race-course. The honourable victory was accorded due accolade by the locals who had watched it train 'up top'. Three days had passed since the great race and still no sign of the hero of the turf. Sunday service started but no one could concentrate on the responses, the parish clerk got a nod from the vicar and took up his position on the spire. A quick clang on the sanctus bell, a breathless shout of "yere is" had the parson closing his book to join his excited congregation in cheering home the pride of Aldsworth's green.

By the turn of the century it was to warn the villagers that the *vicar* was coming that sentinels were posted on the church tower. For many years the rector had to travel from Turkdean, a perilous six miles of up hill and down dales in wild wintry weather. The look-out kept his eye fixed on the northern ridge and as soon as the rector's gig was seen beetling against the skyline the old 'ting-tang' was sounded, bonnets and shawls were hastily donned and the congregation 'skawted off a bit smartish'. No bell, no vicar, no service. Things are different now.

The Leach plays no part in Aldworth's life but skirts the hill to Kilkenny, the 'New Farm' which acquired its Celtic name after Cromwell captured Ireland's Kilkenny in 1650. (How ubiquitous that puritanical ghost still is!)

Downstream is Swyre Farm now home to the Beshara Centre, a very young concept of spiritual orienteering towards working upon oneself based on the more mystical aspect of the Moslem religions. I found the young people there intellectually stimulating and very sincere. And when it came to the local church fête, they were up all night baking bread and biscuits for the stalls.

A dry valley from Aldsworth joins that of the Leach below the promontory of Swyre Farm close to the prehistoric Dean camp site. Then, as if to guard some mystic secret, the Leach goes underground until it has followed the contour of the hill south of Akeman Street, rising again to christen twin villages Eastleach.

Roads knit a pattern through the Eastleaches but the enigma of the Leach is worth a mention here.

Mike Hart's thesis will probably gather cobwebs in the corner of the Bodleian to be sought out only by other academics reading certain aspects of the Cotswolds' physical geography. But many local farmers are anxiously awaiting his findings on why the River Leach behaves in such a strange way along this deeply-cut valley. The Ice Age seems not so far distant when in the lovely Happy Valley, with no sound but water to cause a ripple in the tranquility, Mike pokes strange instruments in the fast flowing stream and takes yet another reading to add to the complexity of digits and dots and dates labelled simply 'data'. The silence makes funny drumming noises and I think it must be the roar of thousands of tons of ice cutting again through the hills as it is carried southwards by the sudden liberation of vast quantities of meltwater. Then all is quiet again until a tractor pants down the track to Macaroni Downs Farm.

Tomorrow the river may have left but a damp memory of its meandering course. Many streams do go underground for short stretches, but the phenomenon of the Leach is that when the rest of the river is in flood, this excessively dry reach from Swyre to the Eastleach Martin road floods also. In a really dry period all is dry. As the discharge of the stream decreases the dry reach lengthens.

Then, as it starts to flow again above ground it is of considerable depth and stagnant. The logical conclusion would be in the make-up of the strata—but any hypothesis on outcrops leaves unanswered why the Coln, which is quite near, does not behave in the same way, and Mike has studied all the Cotswold rivers in scientific detail, being the only person in the country to pursue this particular aspect of geology.

"What bist at then?" asked one old lady through whose garden a Cotswold river was running.

"Monitoring the flow rate," said Mike.

"Oh," she replied, then subjected him to an identification test of various paw marks in the muddy bank. Having failed to distinguish between the prints of a spaniel from those of a sheepdog she snorted in disgust: "What's say you be a'doing?"

"Examining the fluvial geomorphology."

"An thee castn't tell one dog's footprint from t'other—what do 'um larn thee at that university?"

And I thought *Roger Plowman* was invented!

Enchanting Eastleach. Few villages can match its rural simplicity and manage to emit such charm. Here, one feels, is where dinner-time is signalled to the ploughman yonder by a line of billowing sheets hoisted up by a coppice-grown prop. Roads are everywhere, little roads to serve the cottages which cling tenaciously to each shelf of the valley so that garden flowers seem to be toppling out of the very sky. As roads ride the hill at three levels to converge as one parallel to the river, the eye takes in a range of grass-fronted cottages terminating in a clock tower, little 'cots', big 'cots' and cottages all in a row.

This is traditionally Keble Land. In common with other places where he ministered, Eastleach claims to have influenced John Keble's immortal *Christian Year*.

The pastoral beauty of his sacred poetry is everywhere in Eastleach, where only the insentient could feel nothing. The fine clapper bridge, known as Keble's Bridge, would have been crossed by the poet-curate on his way to take divine service in the little church across the water. He would not, as we have, the pleasure of a million golden daffodils bowing and curtseying as we pass by, for they were planted since his day. A curious tale relating how he saved a certain Nellie from an early watery grave seems to survive solely in the realms of a rhyme which I unearthed.

Two churches within nodding distance of each other form a charming focal point and naturally excite romantics into fabricating all sorts of legends to justify their proximity. But their origins are those of every manor when the lord built a church for his own devotions and those of his tenants and servants. The twin villages were united half a century ago; until then each was administered separately on parochial affairs, even to the extent of Eastleach Martin writing to Eastleach Turville (across the stream) asking it to refrain from burying its dead in the other's churchyard.

Eastleach Turville on the west bank is the larger of the two, it is on this side one goes for the bus, butcher, pub and shop and across the bridge to school, which was built on common land by voluntary subscriptions. A schoolroom was formerly close to the river where a Mrs Baxter, in a small black bonnet frilled with Valenciennes lace, "pinned disobedient children to her lilac, besprigged apron".

Eastleach Martin, locally called Bouthrop, wears its antiquity gracefully; scattered along a softly moulded hill it resembles more a settlement than a village proper. Robed and tonsured monks would look just as much a part of the village scene today as they did when the sanctus bell in the lovely old church was first hung and rung. Medieval meditations were not the only murmurings to be heard however. Tempers have flared and riots have reared. What? Gallows at Eastleach! So say the records. And broken by no less a personage than the Abbot of Cirencester who, with others, took away nineteen oxen as well!

Discontent rumbled through the cornfields in later years as machines were installed on the farms. One disorderly mob, driven to desperation by fear and anger, was confronted at Cote Mill by the revered John Keble who, admonishing one fellow for leaving his bootlaces untied, nonplussed the fearsome group who scattered to reassemble another day. November 1830 must have been a noisy month in this quiet corner of the Cotswolds, no cleric could quell the knots of angry men who "riotously and tumultuously assembled together, and then and there did break and destroy several threshing machines," escapades which cost them dearly. Hard labour at the House of Correction in Northleach must have seemed a relief from the transportation sentences which sent their confederates to—records are reticent as to destination. Times were hard and the law severe, fourteen days' hard labour for an Eastleach mason who stole a vest and 'pledged' it for a shilling; a labourer summoned for leaving his employer's service—such accounts punctuate the county court records so it is somewhat a surprise to find the Treasury of Whitehall advertising in *The Times* to seek the next of kin of a John Crook "late of the workhouse Eastleach Turville".

The village owes much to the Bazley family. The present Sir Thomas Bazley is a keen conservationist, congruity of style and natural stone used in recently modernized cottages is the pleasing result. All the crests and clumps and circles of beech and elms and oak, forming such a striking feature of the area between Eastleach and Hatherop, were planted by his grandfather to absorb some of the district's unemployed in the hungry nineties, and the handsome fountain erected in 1874 brought fresh water to the village; a written notice being fixed to the front "to warn the Gibbs' boys of the consequences in case of damage".

It is difficult not to sing the praises of a place one loves. Yet, to do so too loudly will destroy that which is so precious. April brings a flood of visitors to walk beside the daffodil-flanked river where, later, meadowsweet will grow seven feet high. But there is nothing to detain them, other than a quiet drink at the proper country pub. I am fortunate. Eastleach to me is a many splendoured spot—long, sunny afternoons in the beautiful boathouse where time is measured by the clank of a milking bucket, a flurry and flutter of the wild ducks upstream to where Mrs Monk must be calling them for tea and lengthening shadows pointing to my un-finished writing. The dampening grass makes short tearing sounds beneath my feet as I cross the field and call at Bridge Cottage. While the big kettle sings on the shiny black-leaded range Mr Monk talks of vanished village life, charity loaves and Morris dancers, glow-worms and oil-lamps lighting the street, carriers and wheelwrights, the deep freestone mine and little puddled dew-ponds and the fine cress beds from which his grandfather filled the 'flats' to be hawked round the streets of Burford or sent on the old Fairford Flier and on to the Midlands.

A rustle in the thick ivy on the low stone wall signals someone's approach, disturbing the duck which chooses to nest there and the past slips away as a neighbour begs a screw of tea, a dark button or wants medicine collected from Fairford. Every village should have its Bill and Elsie.

The young men used to go to Greenbury House to learn handicrafts in the old laundry in Mrs Fowler's time. I go to learn the local legend from Mrs Honour.

Long days become long weekends in the Tudor cottage further up the hill where the titled and the talented bring the world of the arts into the stimulating atmosphere of the Ustinov household. To the international art academies, the artist whose paintings earned such approbation from Augustus John and the critics, and ballet costume design and theatre decor, is the talented Nadia Benois. Her world-famous son was once referred to as Peter, the son of Nadia Benois. To the villagers she is Mrs Ustinov who would prefer to go with them on a bus, than in state in a taxi, when going to the theatre to see her son's play. To me she is a dear friend who loves the Cotswolds, too.

Southrop is properly called 'Sutherup' so one of its younger in-habitants informed my class. The local children will readily assimi-late the phonetics of a foreign language in their lessons but are adamant when it comes to the speech of their forefathers. Freudi-ans, no doubt would find this aversion to speak 'no posher than our Mum' of immense interest. The intonation of certain syllables obviously still has musical appeal to young ears—'Hatherup, Butherup and Sutherup, all begins with A' is the local anthem.

More serious matters than 'speaking Gloster as she is spoke' were discussed in Southrop Vicarage and brought about the great revival in the Church of England as the young John Keble sowed the first seeds in the minds of his pupils to bear fruition as the Oxford Movement. Local folk are grateful to him for discovering the richly carved font, probably hidden from the Roundhead rascals whose appreciation of the morality behind the carvings would not have saved them on their artistic merit. "Our font was made by the Normans and Walt Sparkes helped make the organ down at Captain Garrad's organ works at Lechdale wharf."

Time matters little along the Leach where the untrammelled sounds of Nature are interspersed by the Cotsall speech of Shakes-peare's day, where simile to the soil or scriptures add colour and cadence and comprehension to everyday life.

The Coln valley starts properly at Wontley Farm near Charlton Abbots. A col provides a good view of the Isbourne flowing north-west along the Postlip Valley to the Avon and the Coln running south-east to the Thames.

Charlton Abbots is watered by two springs, but they, too, show divided loyalties when it comes to direction. High up on the hills, this early monastic village once had a leper's house and still retains an isolated look.

Cotswold mutton and batter pudding would be hardly considered royal fare, but this humble dish was, it is recorded, polished off by 'Farmer George' when His Majesty graciously accepted the invitation to share the family dinner at Brockhampton Park.

Sevenhampton lies in the sweeping hills. A riding school seems a very sound institution if one is to traverse these wildified ways in winter weather. Records speak of snow and ice lingering in the quarries hereabouts until August. In 1634, it's true, but the hills changeth not!

The Shiptons, Solers and Oliffe, speak with the tongue of Cotswold in their name and being. 'Just sin a ship in the strit', might raise many an eyebrow—but not to hill folk to whom 'ship' is not anything to do with sea-faring vessels. In Solers church a punning picture pokes gentle fun at the old Saxon pronunciation. Barns are put to proper use here, and the sound of running water beats a steady tempo through the farmyard scenes.

When Cobbett cantered through woods to Withington he found it "a picture of dilapidation and shabbiness scarcely to be equalled". Motorists picking at barbecued chicken joints in the gardens of the lovely old Mill Inn see the village in a prettier dress. The melancholy decay of last century lingers only within the colourful pages of *Rural Rides*. How the old Radical would have loved to have laid hands on the manuscripts held by the rector, in which a note is added to the minister's Christmas custom of giving to the poor bread, cheese, beer and applepie, "the farmers solicitate for ale instead of small beer that they may drink it all themselves".

I talked to two young women in the church 'like a small Cathedral'. They were going to try their skill at handbell ringing in the winter months. If they put as much vigour in their ringing as they were expending on their polishing the Coln Valley would surely echo.

A footpath winds a dark and secret way to an open field. A short cut for short people was the note I made, for the several little footbridges spanning it would decapitate a scurrying short-sighted five-footer! Winding wooded ways where the road keeps the river within view loop lazily along to Yanworth and tumble down to Fossebridge.

The wooded hollow and water meadows of the Coln's lower reaches must have been known to the Romans. If they chose to overlook it the Normans certainly didn't for their little grey church stands today unsullied and happily unrestored, but the Old Men of the Valley sleep the eternal sleep up on the hill in Colnpen Long Barrow; their successors huddled in round barrows and neighbourly proximity.

Barns and church are roofed alike at Coln St Dennis; as the road dips down from the Fosse Way they appear like a pack of cards pitched ready for shuffling. At one point the church tower appears to be sitting on top of a barn's tallet steps.

"Here lyes my body fast inclosed within this watery ground" laments one memorial. How watery that ground was in those poorly-drained days can still be appreciated by the lushness of the moss and glowing lichens on the stone. A bale of straw and a pile of newly-printed church magazines shared the porch, when I last went there. Divinity is very down-to-earth in our villages.

Calcot, a tiny hamlet, clings bravely to the hillslope which affords good anchorage but little shelter from those lazy Cotsall winds (the ones that go through instead of round you).

Saxon farmers may never have left Coln Rogers, they found fertility in the soil of this valley and raised a church from its matrix in which they could accord their thanks in the same way as their Latin predecessors had raised a temple upstream to the life-giving waters. All is rural, even the remains of a former priest house behind the churchyard wall have been used as a cow-shed.

Winson winds itself winsomely into a prettily packed unit of church, farm, manor and mill and even (if my grandfather's long memory served him faithfully) had its own cricket team, their battle-cry being "together though tired".

This is J. Arthur Gibbs' terrain. One day, I'm sure, the Examination Boards will discover A Cotswold Village and there it will lie, dissected and scattered among the syllabi, to be theorized on by inky-fingered pupils instead of packed into a fishing hamper with a 'snowl' of bread and cheese and delved into beside the weedy, willow-lined Coln.

Piscatorial pilgrims come to Bibury like the medieval monks beat a path to Hailes. Angling seems to have increased with the advent of motoring, the latter taking gentlemen of means to the chalk streams to pursue a less energetic sport than the hawking or hunting which wore their ancestors' seats thin. Now they perch precariously on inadequate stools to get away from the motor—which all accounts for a cousin of Ruskin starting a fish farm here in 1906.

At Bibury, folk pay some kind of continuing homage to the Coln water. On the low wall which separates road from river they sit and watch for a flick of a tail or a flash of a fin. But what a perfect way to idle away an hour. The Swan, where fishermen congregate to tie their flies and tell their lies, looks over its flower-filled garden to the stoutly buttressed mill at Arlington.

Taxidermists stuffed the big ones who didn't get away for old Izaac's disciples to venerate and examples can be seen in the Museum along with an impressive collection of agricultural and domestic implements of yesteryear.

But not all of England's past is committed to the museum's care. Frank Mercer wields a smithy's hammer in the forge close by. This is the heart of hunting country and the demand for a farrier's skill keeps him and his partner and two young apprentices busy in forge and stable from dawn to dusk.

Other echoes from the past are subdued to a name: Rack Isle, a marshy meadow studded with water-loving plants and wild fowl, where cloth was hung to dry on racks after being fulled at the Mill, is edged with England's most famous row of weavers' cottages. Arlington Row has been saved for the nation (and from the ignomy of being exported stone by stone to the United States) by the National Trust. One cottage is to be restored as a weaver's museum, the others are lived in by local people—a fact some curious visitors seem not to realize as they press their noses against the window panes.

The Court, now a hotel, is separated from the village by the church, where old Squire Sackville on seeing the hourglass turned over, and assured by the vicar that the sermon would be only one hour longer, rose from the family pew, went off to "smoak his pipe" and returned in time for the benediction. Rich and wretched share the archives. Television cameras would swoop today on the "poore and impotent Edmond Wilkins" if he had been evicted from the "unfittinge room in the Church house" and enforced with his family of children "to lye in the streets".

It would be as wise to lie in Bibury streets today as to take a nap on the motorway verges as lorries heave their bulky loads along at great speed. The picturesque village which William Morris declared to be the most beautiful in England has been drawn closer to "the madding crowd's ignoble strife" than the gentle Gibbs would have dreamed possible. No wonder the villagers look anxiously at the engineering drawings and models and artists' impressions of the proposed by-pass and wonder what will be murdered in its materialization. Only those whose homes are in this valley should be qualified to select the sacrifice if the road-building gods are to be appeased.

The river, as if to dissociate itself from man's muddling madness, slips along the meadows to Coln Aldwyn where it appears to have undergone some sophistication. Its silvery waters glide gracefully here in contrast to the meditative meanderings of its youthful days upstream in the hills, as though in deference to the disciplined Akeman Street ground into the earth hereabouts by Rome's regimented legions. This is the largest village of the Coln trio. Well-built cottages edge its long street, a wide doorway here, an inset porch there, softening the severity of line as it drops steeply down to where the mill thrusts out a stony corner to narrow the road and check our speed so that the river can be appreciated once more. Thanks to the zeal and skill of Bill Godwin and his merry team, who every Christmas shake the age-old carols out of a clutch of handbells, wring a nostalgic tear and a trickle of silver from the neighbouring wealthy, Coln will soon have the funds to get their church bells pealing once more.

The village stores and a stone-tiled telephone kiosk keep to the crest of the hill, where a lovely chestnut tree stands at the cross-roads like a self-appointed traffic warden and supplies the youngsters with enough 'obblionkers' to rage battle all through the autumn.

Coln, Hatherop and Quenington practically run into each other up and round and down the hill; they share the same vicar, school, Mothers Union, cricket club and W.I.

These slopes are less dramatic than those of the north wolds, Hatherop appears, therefore, more elevated than raised on a hill proper, an eminence heightened by having a castle. The manor and estate of Hatherop, valued at 100 shillings at Domesday, passed through many complicated changes of ownership until Elizabeth I presented it to Sir William Sherington, the nunnery of Lacock being in the same ownership. The Elizabethan manor house was partly rebuilt in the nineteenth century for Lord de Mauley, to be bought by the Government a decade after and leased to the Maharajah Duleep Singh, whose grandson became a world-famous cricketer. In 1870 the estate was bought by Sir Thomas Sebastian Bazley, an M.P. and one of the founders of Manchester University. The Castle was the home of the Bazleys until the last war and became the headquarters of the Danish Resistance. It first became a private girls' school in 1946. It bears no battle scars, no aged line or historic note—no stronghold this.

But let us not pass a village by because our blood is not stirred by bygone tales. History, after all, is but a chronicle of people's doings—and mostly it is only the atrocities or eccentricities that get recorded. Age-old heroics are here reversed for it was the young ladies of the Castle who rescued a knight. Nothing dramatic—a simple act of kindness and concern for others. The schoolgirls 'adopted' one of England's fast dwindling race—a knight of the road. All his life John Charles has tramped the lanes, slept rough and worked at menial tasks for his next meal. Then his tired feet brought him to Hatherop and home. The girls made a collection, bought him a shepherd's hut, painted and furnished it and planted pots of daffodils to brighten the step. Sir Thomas Bazley provided him with a site on his own grounds.

"Lonely? You're never lonely in the country. I've got a good neighbour in Sir Thomas. Ah, yes, folks down village keep talking about Concorde—what is that exactly?"

I explained that it was an areoplane which travelled faster than sound.

"Oh, that's nice," said John Charles and pedalled away on his trike (also presented to him by the girls) to collect the retirement pension for which he is eligible now that he has a permanent address.

Perhaps the story is of no import to posterity any more than future historians will get excited about the scores of quilts and hundreds of cushions which Olia Steiner stitched from silk stars and cotton diamonds into exquisitely designed patchwork. But to this extraordinary nonagenarian the local charities owe a great deal of their funds. Of such simple things from within the woods and behind closed cottage doors the life of a village stems.

Quenington holds my childhood memories fondly in its wide green fields and old grey buildings. Grandparents' homes are of such mystic magic which never dulls, so I can never associate the village as others see it with the place I know it to be. Guides and records and learned writers will tell of its association with the old Knights Templars, an ancient doorway still remains through which they must have passed.

Miles of film must have been expended on trying to capture the vigorous carving on the church doorways. Heaven and Hell lose all traces of nebulosity when interpreted in stone, yet the richly decorated frames are as exactly executed as if embroidered rather than chipped out by mallet and chisel.

Sturdy groups of cottages spread round the wide village green and march down the hill to where the paper-making mill used to work. Despite having a factory in its midst, Quenington retains its rural atmosphere. Hardly a family in the district has not had one of its members apprenticed at Godwin's. About one hundred and fifty local people are employed in this firm which began almost a century ago as an agricultural engineering works concerned mainly with boring for wells. Here and there one still sees Godwin's windmills in a field, but the home and European markets call for highly sophisticated automatic pumps for the industrial, chemical and contractor works. This small country industry now exports all over the world: Nigeria and the Far East have a great demand for the basic 'old-fashioned' pump, so the Quenington windmills are very much a thing of the future in the developing countries.

The absence of any chemical industry on the Coln is the angler's premium.

When the mail coach rattled into Fairford to bring the glad tidings that the Boer War was at an end, it met with but a tardy reception because "the May-fly was up". Today the eyes of the world are on Concorde at its Fairford Test Centre, over the hedge from the tiny village of Whelford. But the keen-eyed angler looks not to the skies as

> Clear Coln and Lively Leche go down
>   from Cotteswold's plain,
> At Lechlade joining hands, come likewise
>   to support
> The mother of great Thames.

II

Churn Valley and Thames Watershed

SEVEN SPRINGS TO LECHLADE

CHURN valley folk claim their river to be the Thames, but it is a local belief rather than a nationally accepted fact. Gurgling and chuckling, the infant Churn bounds away from Seven Springs above Cheltenham at the top of Charlton Kings hill to play around in big puddled ponds in the farms around Coberley.

Claims to fame remain in a name at Coberley. Dick Whittington's mum lies in the church in stately stone, not a bit like we have known her since childhood, but the Lady Joan Berkeley, before she became Lady Whittington through her second marriage, would probably wiggle in her wimple if she knew what stories had been told about her eminent son since those days when they lived in Coberley Hall. That he was brought up by his widowed mother is true. His father, according to the *Inquisitions post mortem* was an outlaw, but this may have been a case of Sir William marrying Sir Thomas de Berkeley's widow without the King's consent. Innocuous enough to society perhaps, but liable to heavy fines on the estate by royal command.

Nothing remains now of the old Hall, but its stones came in useful when new buildings were erected on higher ground above the Hall, the remnants used in the foundations of the road leading from Coberley to Colesbourne upon which the modern road runs. The need to link the newer part of the village to the new road provided a more direct route to Cheltenham, thus cutting out the inconvenient bridle track which went by way of Hartley Bottom to Leckhampton. Short cuts were the order of the day it seems, even the farm horse and cart drove through the church chancel on its way to the mill.

Coberley and Cowley are linked by one of the most attractive parish magazines I have seen. Printed at Coberley Rectory it is packed full of parochial affairs that would adequately answer those inane questions of 'what is there to do in these little villages?' Well, for three days after St Bartholomew's day the yokels took to kicking their neighbours' shins, clobbering them with a cudgell or wringing their limbs—just for fun, of course. But the revellers were found guilty of "very great Enormities in Excessive drinking and unlawful Sports" so the Cowley wake was stopped in 1710.

Social gatherings today are much more refined affairs. Cultural activities, residential courses and educational seminars are centred at Cowley Manor under the auspices of Gloucestershire County Council—the Churn adding charm to the grounds by lurking in lovely lakes and providing a delightful sanctuary for rare plants and birds along its sheltered course. And if the gossip of your neighbours loses its appeal there is always the secret world of the wriggling, winging, singing creatures to be tuned into. Ray Goodwin, a herdsman at Cowley, has caught on tape the conversation of Nature incarnate. His extraordinary collection won him the title of Wildlife Sound Recordist twice in succession and the admiration and respect of every naturalist. Even Lewis Carroll's Alice would have been amazed at Cowley's Wonderland had she known when she visited her uncle here at the Rectory of the male cuckoos who had an off-key singing duel over a female bird, snails munching a lettuce, wasps devouring a mouse carcase, dung beetles at work in a cow pat, hover flies at rest sounding like a factory hooter and of life down a badger hole.

The Churn keeps the main road company down to Colesbourne and one is tempted to disgress a little as it lopes off into the lovely wooded Park. Here, the river hardly moves. Lovely in all seasons, Colesbourne Park is splendid in late autumn when huge, spicy-scented firs 'dout' the flame of gold and copper. A partridge picks its way through summer bleached grass and pheasants see-saw on stone walls while a robin splashes a bare thorn bush with cosy red.

Colesbourne Park has many rare trees from the Himalayas and American forests planted last century by Henry Elwes, one of England's finest arboreal authorities to whom the 2,500 acre estate, now owned by the Western Woodland Owners' Co-operative, owes its magnificent 900-acre Centenary Wood. One of its giant Douglas fir trees now forms the bowsprit for Brunel's steamship S.S. *Great Britain* being rebuilt at Bristol. Mr Henry Elwes, chairman of the company and great grandson of the famous Henry Elwes, gave a number of trees for the ship's new masts.

The little road flanked by copper beech, oaks and holly, spruce and larch, the lesser blackthorns festooned with Old Man's Beard, climbs up into the first reach of the great wooded belt which links the Churn and Coln across the watershed. But the dark waters we now see carrying autumn leaves downstream is the Hilcot Brook. The soil on the opposite bank showed richly red as copper will when needing a polish.

As my eye was drawn up its great slope a sturdy elm crashed and lay like a slain giant across the skyline. Then I heard the saw whining like a funeral dirge and the thin curl of blue smoke which signalled another victim claimed by the elm disease. Perhaps we on the Cotswolds are the more fortunate of Gloucestershire's areas when we learn that there are 158,000 dead elms in the vale. The timber is still commercially viable but not a particularly good one to work; however, its twisting nature adds character to the rustic furniture which many of the county's schools are making for Cotswold picnic areas. Out of the spate of reports on the elm disease which has swept the county is the curious belief that the deadly fungus carried on a beetle's back, by which it infects other trees by burrowing between the bark and the trunk, came over from the continent in elm coffins. But no one has even seen a bark-covered coffin!

Cabbage, wheat, pasture and bracken open out suddenly on the high plateau. Lying in a wooded hollow away to the west, where fungus sprouting from mossy tree roots is a thing of beauty, is Hilcot farmstead, a delightful spot, all rural riverain beloved by its little boys, chicken, sheep and wild ducks.

Back on the main road the Churn is followed closely, affording a fine view of Rendcomb College beautifully situated high up on a green bank. The informed observant will discern the name of Sir Francis Goldsmid depicted in Hebrew characters grown in copses hereabouts. Whatever one reads from such odd egoistic displays the depths of green upon green add yet another facet of charm to this pretty valley.

North Cerney folk have to cross the main road to go to church. Sylphs slip through the narrow wooden stile while others use the lovely lych gate then wait for a strong arm to push open the very heavy oak door. A wealth of detail has been packed into this church to keep glaziers, masons and carpenters busy many long hours. Almost as though there has been some edict issued to preserve here all of import, we find the last words uttered by a Susanna Perry engraved on a little brass, green-fringed with age. Fat cherubs cuddle skulls most unhealthily on one of those memorials that explains who was married to whom who was by whom who died when. That the organ case had once served a hurdy-gurdy gives a homely touch of domestic economy to this place so rich in ecclesiastic treasures.

The pub sign of the 'Bathurst Arms' on the opposite side of the road adds a manorial touch which is otherwise absent from this village and reminds us that Cirencester, seat of the Bathursts, is near.

The ghosts of all history echo along this valley but we have met them before in previous chapters so we need but to nod acknowledgement to the Ancients of Bagendon, the drovers who crossed our path at Perrott's Brook, the Normans at Baunton and the Romans at Cirencester as we hurry on to Siddington and out of the hills. One could argue whether it was even Cotswold, even less a village. So close to Cirencester does it lie that it seems but an extension of that rapidly expanding town.

Over the wall from the busy teeming road horses are schooled over coloured poles, the church spire making a very effective backcloth. Despite its urban encroachments the village retains a pleasant rural atmosphere enlivened by its point-to-point races.

If this were a book devoted to country crafts several chapters would be commanded by spinning and weaving. Thanks to the enthusiasm of Patricia and Arthur Hains of Siddington the fascinating skills and stages which transform the bulky tangled fibres of a fleece into superfine cloth have been taught to local groups. Pat's knowledge of fleeces and dyes, plants and spindles, wefts and warps, teazles and looms, wheels and weights seemed inexhaustible as she patiently went through the basic processes for me. The dye labels on wool overflowing from wooden trugs read like an eighteenth-century cookery book: young rhubarb leaves, marigold, onion skins, apple, walnut, nettle tops. She admitted that while cooking she is sometimes tempted to experiment with yet another plant or stone or paring. "Often," she laughed, "the children lift a lid in the kitchen asking what's for lunch—ugh, bracken!"

I was thrilled to see that she folded and rolled and bound up the fleece in the traditional Cotswold fashion as practised down the centuries just as though this was all part of today's way of life.

A charter dated 1558 *Inspeximus*, by Philip and Mary, refers to the "Customes and Constitutions of the craft and occupacion of Weavers in the Towne of Cisceter" as being "of olde antiquitie out of tyme and mynde".

> God loveth sinners
> Dyers and spinners
> Weavers even
> May hope for heaven
> When naught is left
> Of warp and weft,
> With spindle and loom
> They will meet their doom.
> The lamb's white fleece
> Has brought their peace.

Whether that was meant to afford spiritual comfort to the weavers who suffered most by the introduction of machinery is possible. Certainly in these mechanical driven days the old crafts are of therapeutic as well as aesthetic value. The amazing thing is that their revival, albeit carried on in a cottage here or a back yard there, is stimulated by a sense of discovery, so that a reconstruction of a loom of the neolithic appears strangely neoteric.

A local landmark is a round house which is identified as a windmill on a map of 1824; in the County Records Office a lease refers to a wind grist mill in Siddington built by the Earl Bathurst so it is possible that when the sails were removed the battlements were added.

South Cerney means water, but it is the waters from under the earth appearing in great glassy lakes which are the attraction here to water sports enthusiasts. The inhabitants have plenty of other pursuits in this busy thriving village to keep them happy. The local drama and arts groups are well acclaimed, there is a variety of sports clubs and a very active Trust which keeps an eye on the context of the village and plants flowers along the footpaths.

There is no shortage of work here where the Cotswold limestone meets the gravel of the Thames watershed and in a way one is supplementing the other. The increased demand for concrete and reconstituted stone has meant a new kind of mining; as the gravel is extracted the deep pits fill with water.

A Bronze Age man lost his spearhead here some 3,000 years ago where, when the sun sets over the water, I feel I have heeled back to Genesis. In some ways I don't think the village has changed since my grandmother's day, folks still take a pride in their allotments and no one has changed the name of Bow-Wow, that lovely old walk. Lollipop men are a new feature necessitated by the volume and ferocity of the gravel lorries, while the carrier has been relegated to memory. But I think it must have been a very leisurely mode of travel because I remember my grandmother saying that her neighbour, when 'skawting' off into Cirencester said, "I can't stop for a lift today, Mr Gassor, I'm in a terrible hurry."

Agriculture has dwindled as land is eaten into for gravel but the farmer has not been cast aside for manufactory; block-makers, engineers, gardeners, cartographers, farmers and pipe makers each have their place in South Cerney where the ancient observance of Plough Sunday has been recently revived.

Cartographic Services, one of only a dozen such firms in the whole country, was originated by Mr Yeates a local man and has been centred at South Cerney since 1965. A staff of twenty process all types of maps, principally for the educational world and particularly for the emerging countries of the Far East and Africa, along with the guide book, road map, conservation map and school atlas. It was intriguing to know that those wiggly lines and symbols, demanding the ultimate in artistic and creative skill for camera reproduction and plate-making by the most modern techniques, could be translated into twisted lanes and sweeping hills and tucked away villages.

I suppose a future map will have big blue splodges along this Thames watershed as gravel pits are developed into lakes. Progress is made yearly and eventually all lakes will be embraced by the Cotswold Water Park which will stretch from South Cerney's already established Marina to the head of Thames Valley at Lechlade. Roads will run between the lakes which cannot, as some folk fear, merge and flood us all out of the south-east Cotswolds owing to the different heights of the water tables.

Driffield's water is a much more local affair—a real duckpond where black and white ducks dawdle away their time and sparrows fuss hurriedly to peck cautiously at its edge. To this village, which time seems to have passed by, a nephew of John Hanger came to escape the plague rampaging in London. 'Blue Hanger', the fourth Lord Coleraine, has a carefully worded epitaph which indicates a frail nature but other works tell the tale of how notorious George's "eccentric manners became too free and coarse even for the Prince Regent". Prey to superstition he, as other rakes of that age, requested a burial above ground so that the devil wouldn't get him—his coffin was later placed underneath the organ.

The community numbers less than a hundred today, about the same as in the Middle Ages when it was held by Cirencester Abbey. Tradition claims this to be the resting place of its last abbot.

Harnhill was formally joined to Driffield parish in 1882, three hundred years after the parishioners first petitioned the Bishop of Gloucester to do so—"being but a furlong apart". It could have meant that Harnhill folk hoped to have Driffield's vicar oust their own "suttel man", who was also "an untrew man, a crafty fellow and a perjured man".

A village wedding is always an important event; a wedding at Harnhill is of great importance: to date only forty-seven brides have walked down its church aisle since registers were first kept.

The four Ampneys (silent p) are each a parish and village. Ampney Crucis, the first of the trio approached from Cirencester leads off the old London coach road where less hurried travellers stopped to have their steeds shod at the seventeenth-century forge. The village itself nestles back from the main road between stone walls, and could easily escape the notice of a speeding motorist for the inn leads the eye on along the busy main road. Turning to the left we immediately reduce our tempo of thought as well as speed: the calmness of the silvery water in which the sixteenth-century mill is reflected, its wheel now still, its walls untouched by the renovator, is the perfect anodyne to the twentieth-century traveller.

The pride of owning one of the most famous old crosses in England belongs to Ampney Crucis. Another cross, lichened and sadly worn, is but five hundred years old and was built up in the church to save it from destruction until it was brought out into the light again last century.

This is Saxon country; their hands laid the long-and-short masonry in the church and their conquerors embellished it with one of the finest chancel arches in the Cotswolds. A scratch dial on the south porch would have told the villagers the hour they went into this tree-shadowed church, which Domesday records as Omenie Holy Rood, and many a wary eye must have watched the hourglass as the sermon grew longer and the old pews harder.

Here is the culmination of a thousand Sunday evenings, rustling silks and homespun shawls weaving their way through the centuries and the lengthening churchyard shadows, but beneath that placid portrait there beat some angry hearts in answer to the Word as preached by their vicar, Benedict Grace, whose very name was para-doxical to his character.

This was no disgruntled flock muttering between the tombstones after an unpleasant sermon, this was "the inhabitants of Holyrood Ampney in the County of Gloucester" presenting a "humble peti-cion in the Honourable House of Commons in the high Court of Parliament bearing date the 19th day of December 1640". Benedict Grace, they claimed, was "scandelous, persecuting, quarrelsome, bold, uncivill and ignorant Minister. Scandalous, in that he is given to drunkeness and Lechery, persecuting, in that he commenceth very many and more unjust suits, quarrelsome in that he hath been the author of many frayes and Actor of more assaults, bold in that he threatens his parishioners with complaynts to the Archbishop of Canterbury, and preaching other mens Sermons. Uncivill, in that he useth fifthy language to all sorts of people, ignorant, in that he Wants Learning . . . and humbly pray the remoovall of him".

A letter of 1641, referring to this graceless Grace, says, ". . . he tooke occasion to speak very scandalousely touchinge the pro-cedings of the Parliament agaynst the late Lorde Straford, offering they had malitiously put him to death. I finde he acknowledged his name was Grace, and by all surcomstances it was yowre mynnes-ter".

Parish politics is one thing, parliamentary politics another. Well, well! Who would have thought such goings on went on in this lovely old village. The not very reverent Benedict Grace seems to have earned his living from the parish, and contempt from his parishioners, until 1670.

Situated between Fairford and Cirencester, both embroiled in the Civil War, Ampney Crucis did not totally escape involvement as the records, suddenly reticent about the political parson, contain entries of burial of two "soldiers for the King".

There is an abundance of historical treasure in the stone that shapes this village, no less than fifty buildings are officially scheduled as being of special architectural or historic interest, but it is the simple complexity of parochial affairs where one feels an integral part of the community which makes village life so special, as when Ampney held a festival last year and we could boo the vicar's runs and cheer the ladies' in a comic cricket match. Holding one's breath in case an 'Ampney Belle' missed her turn and shook her handbell in the wrong spot, relaying weather reports to the organizers, feeling as proud of Mr Barnes's beautifully carved models of a spindle-sided bow waggon, hurdles and kissing gates as if we had been the carpenter, smiling knowingly when visitors remarked on the rosiness of the Ampney Red apple—for we know it to be 'as sour as varges' being a cider apple—clapping madly when Jason completed the intricate ins and outs of dancing round the maypole right way round—of such things is a village honour upheld.

Along the A417 we could hear the rumble of Ampney mill if we slowed down and paused a moment. One of the few surviving mills, it has been worked by Mr Stalworthy and his son continuously since 1928, and has been in the family for over a century.

"I remember these bins all full," said young Mr Stalworthy. "I suppose one day it will become a home for some wealthy newcomer."

I hope not. It is a mill put to proper use, completely water driven, the handles of the wooden sack trucks polished by the hands of generations, lovely mealy hessian sacks, leather straps—probably from a discarded harness—as hinges for the trap door to let sacks up through the floor and prevent the miller falling down. Serving a radius of some twelve miles, it affords work now for only two men.

A new stretch of road beckons us on. An imposing chestnut tree stands on a grassy island; leafy arms direct the fast-moving traffic each side of it like a venerable old policeman on duty. But it's a trick, evolved through a law older than that of dual carriageways.

Why does Ampney St Mary have to be sought out? It has even renounced its former name as though to escape detection.

Authorities differ in their accounts of bereaved Ampney St Mary, *née* Ashbrook. The answer lies buried in the former village, sleeping around the lonely little church to your right. There is no roadway to it. A worn track beside the churchyard wall skirts a field and leads us, muddy-footed, to the old gate. A hare, lolloping across the meadow, pauses and raises itself on its haunches, its nose twitches nervously at our audacity, and then, as though confident in the sentinel might of the two elms guarding the entrance, it disappears in a flash of tawny fur. When lit by a hundred candles last Christmas for a charming concert by Peter Griffiths of Ampney Crucis and Colin Howard the little Ivy Church had more close-packed holiness than ever possible in a large cathedral. The vicar let us clap our appreciation—it helped to scare away the field mice who nest in the nave and kept our hands warm, and I wondered about those early villagers.

The tombstones are not ancient, but what of those to whom no monument was raised? What stilled the hand of the black-smith? What 'douted' his fire? Was it another, all-consuming, blaze as Cirencester was taken in the Civil War, or was it the cold hand of the Black Death that razed the village which once stood where only meadows and silence are now? Those Cotsallers, who worshipped in this little church when the blues and greens of the wall paintings were as bright and fresh as the sky and grass outside, sleep with their secret. A more peaceful end came, we hope, to the Norman mason who shaped the font, and his fellow craftsmen who raised in stone the lion devouring round-headed serpents in the tympanum on the outside north wall, an ancient symbol of good conquering evil.

Superstition prevented rebuilding on the site of the old village. Across the road between leafy lanes is the new Ampney St Mary. Some of the older inhabitants recall the Ashbrook Feast which was celebrated every July. The village straggles its way into a by-road which will take the traveller northwards into Quenington or southwards to join again the main road.

Ampney St Peter is a cul-de-sac of lovely Cotswold cottages standing in simple charm. It is not a showplace for the tourist. It belongs to its people therefore retaining the quiet dignity of a place known to villagers long before man fashioned the stone under his feet to shelter his head, for close by is Ranbury Ring Camp, once an important Roman earthwork.

The Saxons left legacies here in their stonework to be followed by the skill of their conquerors. Names linger on in this delightful homely cluster: the village pub, the Packhorse Inn, was serving ale to dusty travellers as Charles II was restored to the throne.

Older folk still refer to this village as Eastington, its original name. Few now recall the Banbury cakes, the sticky buns and laughter echoing through a July Sunday at Eastington Feast; even fewer remember washing clothes and pigs' chitterlings in "Splash", the extra water from the Ampney brook, called variously the Shire or Share brook; and none remember the annual bidding for Church Ground while an inch of candle burned. It is an old charity of two acres of land which was let for a year to the highest bidder. The proceeds were devoted by the churchwardens to church expenses. The land is still let, devoid of the ancient custom, but for the same purpose.

Down Ampney stands apart from the other Cotswold Ampneys. As though in concession to its near neighbour, Wiltshire, some of the seventeenth-century cottages sport shaggy thatched roofs in contrast to the traditional stone slates. The Ampney trio, closely related in position and style, are like friendly cousins to whom one enjoys an informal visit. They are homely, warm, and welcoming, whereas approaching Down Ampney is like visiting a rather strict aunt in her prim drawing-room.

When Leland came through this part of the Cotswolds he recorded in his small handwriting, "Amney brook riseth a little above Amney Town by North out of the rock. Sir Antony Hungerford hath a fair house of stone." No doubt this itinerant traveller watered his horse, as many have since been watered, at the stone trough which still stands on the side of the Cirencester road opposite the long high boundary wall of Ampney Park.

Today's traveller will find Down Ampney on a series of bends on the winding road that joins the nearby Swindon road, hissing and snarling with heavy milk tankers on their way to and from the great C.W.S. creameries at Latton. It is a village with neither pub nor post office nor central point.

All Saints is a graceful church in a graceful setting. Influential inhabitants are immortalized here: Sir Anthony Hungerford is remembered in gilded letters, stone effigy and the rebuilding of the beautiful mansion; Sir Nicholas Villiers rests beside his daughter, stone figures with stone dogs at their feet, the last Crusade fought and the helping hand to the Knights Hospitallers stilled.

The village has two stone memorial crosses, one very ancient could be marking the spot of an historical meeting? Claim has been laid on behalf of Down Ampney for it being the venue to which St Augustine travelled to meet the British bishops on a momentous day in 603.

There is no such conjecture about the place whose son was that most English of composers, Ralph Vaughan Williams, for if one didn't go into the church where his father had preached to find the memorial to him depicting the Resurrection, his birthplace has been recorded for posterity in that stirring hymn 'Down Ampney'.

When as estate such as Poulton Priory comes up for sale, everyone in the locality gets interested, not as potential purchasers—with an average £1,319 an acre few could afford to be *that* interested, but we scan the local papers and listen to local speculation as to what is to be inflicted on our corner of the Cotswolds. And we sigh with relief when we are told it is 'just for living in', and glad that Poulton will have a bit of the land under the will of the late Major Mitchell on which to build a new school.

Primary Schools hereabouts all seem to have had an anniversary in 1972: Poulton pupils went back to school in the Christmas holidays and banged drums, tolled the bell and knocked the walls a hundred times to celebrate their centenary; Ampney Crucis is somewhat a veteran, being founded in 1722, probably the oldest in Gloucestershire; 'school' was originally lessons taught in a barn.

Meyseyhampton celebrated their centenary by planting a flowering cherry tree as a permanent reminder—the lovely birthday cake was but a sweet memory a few minutes after it had been cut; even the school hamster had a taste.

I recall going on a walk one hot Sunday afternoon with the dogs of Meyseyhampton—the whole pack of the VWH foxhounds, and learnt a great deal of them from the Master of the Hunt. On a densely foggy November afternoon I learnt much of the skill of a master farrier from Frank Mercer. How proud those hunters would have been, I'm sure, if they but knew their shoes were being fashioned by the same hands which made all the shoes for the British team when they won the Gold Medal at the Mexico Olympics. A tiny microcosm of traditional English life, played out in the Kennels which had grown from the hieroglyphics on a blue-print in my Pop's old trunk of long ago.

Once upon a time Lechlade children could recite Shelley's lines which he wrote in the churchyard, today they are better-versed in Concorde's latest test speeds and soon it will be the cult of the water-heroes at the Cotswold Water Park.

Poetry of the Painswick Valleys

COATES—WHITEWAY—OWLPEN

LECHLADE has always been on a crossroads of water. Canal enthusiasts might well weep their way along the neglected route of the Thames and Severn Canal from Lechlade, back along the Thames watershed and westwards into the Golden Valley. Such pilgrims will pay their respects and quench their thirst at Tunnel House set back in the woods at Coates, a couple of miles west of Cirencester.

The inn, built by one of the Lords Bathurst, was originally called the New Inn and the landlord was paid to keep a check on the men, a difficult task if he was to make a living out of his trade as well! The first man engaged to build the tunnel seems to have been a hard drinker and was eventually arrested for "not letting Doorbar Timber the roof".

Tunnelling has always exacted its toll and many men lost their lives fulfilling the plan laid by the poet Pope and financed by the Lord Bathurst. Vivid and lurid are the tales handed down about the old 'leggers' who had to propel their barges through the long tunnel by 'walking them through upside down'. The population of Sapperton and Coates increased considerably as a result of the mining men marrying local girls and settling in the Cotswold parishes. Footpaths from Coates and Tarlton meet at Tunnel House, the only pub between the two villages.

Again, it was in the most unlikely of the Cotswold villages that I discovered country craftsmen. Coates has its wheelwright, next door to a garage, and a thatcher in a council house.

I can imagine the look of surprise David White attracts as he arrives to start thatching a roof. No doubt expecting to see a venerable old man who has pottered back from retirement to practise his skills as a kind of craftsman's swan-song, the customer is confronted by an extremely young man with long curly black hair blowing in the breeze, whose talent, skill, dedication, enthusiasm—call it what you will—is evident in his work. He is, as the old craftsman from whom he learnt the craft, a perfectionist. I was fascinated by the language of the thatcher and the intricacies of the art, and was amazed to learn that a few new houses are being built specifically for a thatch. When one realizes that about four-and-a-half tons of reed goes into thatching one cottage, the rafters have to be somewhat substantial.

The valleys nurture their craftsmen and their poets, the Golden Valley and the Painswick Valleys and all the little combes between make a natural cell where art and thought can flourish and flower. W. H. Davies, while living at Nailsworth, knew these valleys and their secrets and bade us make time "to stop and stare".

Rodmarton Manor is held up as an example of a pure revival of local architecture instead of a slavish imitation of it—the result is a genuine style created for the particular site and situation entirely hand wrought by local craftsmen. No greater memorial could be accorded to Ernest Barnsley, the architect, than this superb country house, gabled, gracious and truly Cotswold. No finer epitaph could be accorded to the Hon. Claud Biddulph than "the improvement of the property and the welfare of the villagers were his life's work".

The village itself is testimony to the tradition of careful workmanship and people who care about the place as a home, not as an investment in the tourist trade.

Rodmarton was home to Samuel Lysons to whom the discovery of Woodchester's Roman settlement was due, and despite his interest in antiquities leading him to the position of keeper of the muniments of the great city, it was those of his native county which appear in his great *Gloucestershire Collection* of customs and monuments and buildings. His own memorial is in the parish church which is famous for its tea-caddy-shaped tombs. A good old-fashioned stile still points the way folks would have taken to Cherington when walking was a necessity.

Cherington demands a slower tempo. Its lake is all that a village lake should be, wild, unkempt—well, that depends who is looking at it and why. If 'lake' conjures up a picture of clear water with plastic-covered boats bobbing up and down, flags flying and ice cream booths at judicious intervals—then seek not Cherington lake where wagtails use the great flat leaves of the waterlilies as stepping stones, bullrushes and ragged robin and a thousand water-loving plants fringe the edges of the dark, still water over which dragonflies dart and carry a spark of sunlight into the deep woods beyond; where tiny gnats spiral over the meadowsweet, dog roses ramble, yellow vetches scramble, and the anglers take not the fish away.

All much about the same as when the monks of Llanthony Abbey came here to collect their dues. The gallows on the tump at the top of Lake Road have gone and the school is now no more, but the village generally seems impervious to change. Though I do believe the age-old feud between Cherington and Avening no longer exists. Certainly they have stopped pinching each other's church bells at night.

Nags Head hamlet has lost its pub but Nen remembered where to find the spring. How bright and cold that irony tasting water is bubbling out of the limestone. We wandered up the hill to Barrow Tump and along the grassy lane where gypsies used to camp when Tetbury Show was the great social occasion hereabouts and caught the sounds of life in the cottages on the opposite bank.

Avening keeps its traditions alive but has not settled into the past. Queen Matilda, wife of the Conqueror, is honoured today by 'Pig's Face' sandwiches served in the local inns on Avening Feast day, not at all a deprecatory dish but a reminder of how, amidst all the pomp and circumstance surrounding the royal patroness who founded the living, she and her entourage feasted on the humble meat and brawn before the awe-stricken villagers.

To Avening House the county schools send little parties for residential courses. I wonder what the children will remember in years to come. Will it be the big country house with its sweeping grounds, cricket in the buttercup field beyond, day-time rambles looking for ferns and wild strawberries, midnight rambles into the beech woods to watch for badgers, crowding into the village shop and buying up the entire sweet stock, or watching at Longford's Mill the weaving of the scarlet cloth for which the

Stroud valley is famous. Badgers, adders and beech wooded combes, tingle stone and barrow, ghosts and legends all clamour for attention of heart and eye.

Minchinhampton celebrates its status as a market town by holding proper country-style fayres where roasting ox and Morris dancing bring a flavour of Merrie England to its streets. Cattle and horses have roamed Minchinhampton Common long before Tom Long, the notorious highwayman, had his bones laid there, and take to the little township when in search of shelter or shade. Enterprising residents who reject 'fertility stuffs' for their rose beds keep a bucket and shovel handy. Most people seem to look on these incursions with affection even if the cattle take a fancy to the paint on the front door and lick it off! But Committees have noticed. And 'Grids' have been mentioned. The most startling suggestion from an opinion poll taken from townsfolk who, to survey nature, crowd on to the Common in close-parked cars, was that public conveniences should be erected at a central point and cattle and horses banned during the summer months!

The signboard of the Blue Boys Inn, Minchinhampton, a posting house for the London coach until 1866, is preserved in Stroud Museum. What is of interest, apart from the pictorial presentation of dyers with their vat, is the veiled political message contained in the motto:

> Tho' we stand here in wind and rain
> True Blue will never stain

Innuendos in the indigo?

The Cotswolds are particularly rich in churches, the churches richly endowed with stained glass, and the exciting thing is that some of those glowing scenes were created by a Cotswold artist in the tiny scattered village of Box. What a fascinating craft, what a true craftsman is Edward Payne.

Not all Cotswold's art is so easily seen: the great Roman pavement at Woodchester, unmatched by any Roman mosaic north of the Alps in both size and degree of elaboration, is revealed to public view but once every decade. Each excavation extends farther afield and spades probe deeper into history. By the end of August 1973 over 140,000 people had gazed down upon Orpheus charming the wild creatures. Now they lie beneath hundreds of tons of brown earth, the best proven method of preserving the mosaic,

M

until the mammoth task of organizing the next 'dig' is again final-ized.

Amberley stands on the edge of the great plateau; high, exposed and scattered as if by the four winds; while Chalford straggles along the valley bottom and up into the shelves of the facing hills. Locally known as Neddyshire on account of donkeys being the principal form of transport, the railway, river and remains of the old canal are crossed by the road along the valley floor. The woollen industry has moved away from Chalford but many modern in-dustries have developed in their place.

The age of the golden fleece gave this area the much disputed appellation of the Golden Valley (a name officially designated to the run between Gloucester and Cheltenham) however, it is a fit-ting choice in autumn when Sapperton woods gild the valley with gold and red, bronze and copper, orange and yellow. I like to think that the Poet Laureate, John Masefield, packed some of Sapper-ton's countryside into his poems.

At the head of the valley it escaped the industrial net of the western edge and is remembered as the centre of fine craftsman-ship: Jewson, Gimson, Waal and the brothers Barnsley are names too eminent in the greatest craft tradition to bear repetition and fresh appraisal.

The church is peopled with effigies of the Poole family, a little lady leans her elbow in the most engaging picture of boredom be-hind Lady Poole and brings a touch of humanity to the pompous poses. Sir Robert Atkyns, county historian, reclines at the other end of the church.

Daneway House, a mellowed medieval many-gabled gem of Cots-wold architecture, was the great craft workshop. Daneway Inn was once the 'Bricklayer's Arms' and served the builders at this end of the tunnel.

Snow-clad Frampton Mansell could be an alpine village with its continental-styled church. From one point on the opposite hill one can look right through the tower apertures. But there is no mistaking its Cotswold lineage in other seasons.

Springs gush out of the hillside and tumble headlong over roots and road to be caught by the Frome in the bottom as the road winds up to Oakridge. Bicycles are very rarely seen hereabouts, papers are delivered on prams.

Far Oakridge has a fine leatherworker. The Visitors' Book used by the Queen at the opening of the Severn Bridge was made here by Theo Merrett who had won the Godsell Cup while at Art College. One of his most exacting commissions was rebinding Dame Edith Sitwell's early volume of Shakespeare's works, dated 1632. Artistically, it presented no problem to this versatile craftsman who can bind books, restore maps, design and make leather cases to fit anything and frame pictures, but the responsibility of working on a folio valued at £17,000 must have been a headache.

Miserden is Cotswold at its neatest, no straw, no farmyard mess; the village tucks itself tidily along one of these streets which has a twist in it to add a vestige of privacy to its houses while the Park hides away in spectacular seclusion where the Black Prince came to the wooded lake to court his Fair Maid of Kent. Above the deep wooded valley of the Holy Brook is the lovely Cotswold home of Pat Smythe, the world-famous horsewoman who pioneered show-jumping for us in the international field.

Whiteway to the north is not an old-established village but was founded in 1898 by a group of people who built their own houses and lived a self-supporting life according to Tolstoyian principles. It is an obvious spot for craftsmen, but out of the dozen or so furniture-makers that were in this area twenty years ago only one remains, the rest seem to have been pushed down to Gloucester Trading Estate.

When the Gimson workshops which had moved to Chalford burnt out, the craftsmen spread out into the villages. Gradually the old Gimson crowd around Water Lane died out or else went into antiques—the only way to get individuality. There is now a trend to reverting back to hand-made furniture again as a means of acquiring individuality now that the antique market has been exploited. I found Peter and Joy Evans working at their crafts quite happily on a Sunday. How stimulating and marvellous these craftsmen are whose values are not measured in terms of cash. Joy does the wood carving using the off-cuts which Peter can't use in his furniture. Their combined skills and personal involvement restore one's faith in man's ability to work with nature once again.

In this world of immediate plastics it is certainly encouraging to find these true artists who have to look forward some fifteen years when selecting wood, which never ceases to be an organic entity. The Tolstoyian ethos is still in evidence. Originality extends to using a hearse for transporting their lengths of timber; they enjoy the obvious respect this commands from passers-by, "but," Peter assured me, "we make a point of not using it when making a delivery to a customer."

Cranham's beauty is its woods—glowing, gleaming beech woods. The Cranham Enterprise, recently launched, is a 'village-to-village' scheme for conservation. Several acres of land have been donated by local people to be used as future nurseries for young trees awaiting transplanting to transform the slag heaps of South Wales, the Midlands or the North into wooded slopes.

It is generally believed that Gustav Holst composed the Christmas carol, 'In the Bleak Mid-winter' to the tune 'Cranham' in a cottage in the village.

The Englishman's passion for pageantry and his penchant for telescoping the centuries has resulted in the revival of Cranham Feast: olde-worlde fun-making is the order of the day on this ancient festival which originated with beating the parish bounds.

Over at tiny Randwick the folk-lorists are well catered for by the Wap: mock-mayor making has an intricate history and visitors are mystified at what the Cotsallers do with the famous Double Gloucester cheese, for here three are rolled around the churchyard then sent spinning down a steep slope to signal the opening of the village stalls.

The Painswick Valleys are sheer poetry, out of which Painswick itself rises majestically to be accorded the title of Queen of the Cotswolds.

Like her attendant villages, Painswick grew up on the wool-trade. Like them, too, the rumble of machinery sounded the death knell to the small water-powered mills, but Painswick has survived the traumas of each age. Even the early Lords of the Manor seemed to have been denied the comfort of dying in bed: battles, suicide, accidents, murders—all plucked them off; one tragically died of relief when he was told of his impending release from imprisonment in the Tower.

The church, a fitting centrepiece to the village, bears scars from the Civil War and German bombers destroyed many buildings which had been erected by the wealthy mill owners. Life, too, was lost in those raids. Now the centre of the Gloucestershire Guild of Craftsmen, Painswick is a thriving nucleus of crafts and what artist or photographer has not captured the village itself from the hills of the south-east by Bull's Cross, where it appears as a jewel caught in the patchwork of the countryside.

Painswick Beacon is beloved by everyone, an absolute paradise for young children who can follow little trackways leading in and out of the bushes. Ardent hikers will make use of the well sign-posted paths while others just look and linger. From this spot Charles I watched his soldiers advance on Gloucester and to this spot, high up on a wooded spur, the Royalists returned some time after and camped the night. The young Prince of Wales asked his father if they could go home; "My son, we have no home," replied the weary King.

Coming down from the Beacon and taking refuge in the tiny hamlet deep in a wooded combe, the King is said to have exclaimed: "This is paradise." So, Paradise it is—and woe betide those who try to change its name, as past experience has proved.

The inn (formerly the 'Plough') on the sweeping road above Paradise is appropriately renamed the 'Adam and Eve'. Belonging at one time to Godsell's Brewery of Salmon Springs prompted the local ditty:

> The Adam and Eve Inn,
> Paradise,
> God sells beer!

Contiguous to the grounds of Paradise House are magnificent conifers said to have come from the Holy Land. Certainly, the charming pastoral little spot is appositely named.

The monastery of the Cotswolds is Prinknash, Horace Walpole saw it "standing on a glorious but impracticable hill, in the midst of a little forest of beech, and commanding Elysium." A modern building, imposing in golden stone, some 2,500 tons quarried from Guiting, now dominates its thousand years' history. Sheltered from the east winds by encircling hills, it commands wide views towards the nebulous looking Malverns and west to the snow-capped Black Mountains. The vicissitudes of monastic life were suffered here as elsewhere but the Benedictine monks returned to the old ancestral home in 1928—the sign outside the Abbey is large and welcoming. Prinknash pottery is known the world over, it is a fascinating community where farming and embroidery are carried on alongside an incense industry.

Busy Bisley, unpretentious and historical. Here are the seven springs which have been issuing forth for the use of the villagers since the Iron Age. Each Ascension Day the colourful ceremony of Dressing the Wells attracts hundreds of visitors to this pagan custom which was revived and christianized by the Rev. Thomas Keble, younger brother of the famed John Keble. Tom Keble, as he was affectionately known, left no stone unturned in helping his parishioners, not by charity but by creating employment whereby they retained their self-respect. Poverty and plague were combated by every method he could devise.

Slad hasn't changed too much since Laurie Lee captured its rural charm and characters into his recollections of *Cider with Rosie*. Fame has not severed his affections for the valley of his childhood. The 'Woolpack' is a kind of haven to which his admirers flock hoping to catch a snatch of the broad rolling speech of the Stroud tongue; if they're lucky they might see the poet himself with the villagers he wrote about. Sly winks are exchanged between the locals if one mentions the precocious 'Rosie' in this *vade mecum* of Slad, where carol services and harvest festivals are held in its cosy bar. 'Cider Rosie' is a Slad valley cocktail which would be a new concoction to appease the visitor. But all else faithfully adheres to the rustic image—the pond is still derelict and wonderfully wild, an old piebald roams the rambling fields and an ancient goat is tethered close to a cottage.

Fog gathers swiftly in these valleys, stone pillars loom up suddenly out of the mist, ghosts and legends swirl crazily, too, around the rambling countryside. Lypiatt lurks in the memory as the place where the Gunpowder Plot was hatched, and a little boy recited to me the epitaph to a horse which he says he saw in the Manor grounds:

> My name is Wag
> Who rode the green
> The oldest horse even seen
> My age it numbered forty-two
> And I served my master just and true.

Many hamlets stud these wooded combes, and such a number of erstwhile villages seem to run into that 'strewed' bit of Bisley that has amassed itself into the township of Stroud that it seems a good idea to take to the plateau on top of the hills to the south-west at Nympsfield and orientate anew. Better still, of course, to soar above the countryside in a glider from the Gliding Club.

Nympsfield, too, was tied to the weaving trade by the frail thread of industry but one would never suspect that the hub and thump of looms and the splash and clack of mills were once throbbing away in the tree crowded clefts below, nor that the placid spot of Horsley across yonder had once bred a beater-up of Tax-collectors.

And suddenly, I came upon Owlpen following the famous directions of old Ferribee as "first you go down Fiery Lane until you come to Cuckoo Brook, then go to Horn Knep and round by Dragon's Den, carry on until you come to Potlid Green and so to Marling's End. If you keep straight on you will come right in to Olepen, but you must take care not to miss the road." The innkeeper told no lies, though it is but a mile from Uley. I had sought a ghost but found a dream. It is not a village as such—and yet it is as complete a unit as any. A small gabled Manor, open to the public at mid-summer, a church, a barn, a mill and court-house, stretching along an unbroken descent of some twenty-two generations, spanning eight centuries. Its history demands too much space, its ghosts suddenly seem insignificant for this setting. On the hill above, but a shadow remains of the Victorian mansion, while neglected Owlpen down in its dell faded but never died. Norman Jewson, Gimson's collaborator, revived its Cotswold architecture and it stands today as testimony to all things Cotswold.

But the Cotsall tongue, albeit only at Christmastide from those charming Waterley Bottom Mummers, shall be allowed the final word in the Saxon greeting:

Wassail!

Postscript

It is perhaps worth mentioning here that a long-distance footpath, called the Cotswold Way, has been created by the Gloucestershire County Council following a route first suggested by the Ramblers Association some twenty years ago.

Fully waymarked by the Cotswold Wardens (a volunteer service formed when the Cotswolds were designated an area of outstanding natural beauty) and the Ramblers, using the first signposts in the country to show distances in kilometres, the route follows existing rights of way from Bath to Chipping Campden.

For almost one hundred miles the footpath is drawn out beside rippling streams and silent quarries, over rustic footbridges and 'oont'-ridden hillocks, through quaint 'kissing' gates and rustling beech woods, alongside whispering cornfields and golfers' fairways climbing steeply and descending sharply while following the dramatic escarpment for much of the time.

A northward direction offers the added attractions of having the prevailing south-westerly weather to one's back and the character of the Cotswolds scenery unfolding ahead. Climbing out of Bath by way of Kelston Round Hill the route takes in Tormarton and the Sodburys, Nibley Knoll and Stinchcombe Hill, Frocester and Haresfield Beacon, Painswick Hill Fort, Cooper's Hill and Birdlip, by the Devil's Chimney high up on Leckhampton to the highest point of the Cotswolds at Cleeve Cloud, descending to the ancient Mercian capital of Winchcombe and historic Hailes, climbing to Beckbury Camp, dipping down to Stanway and Stanton, Broadway and on to Chipping Campden, punctuated by antiquities in the shape of long barrows and round barrows and hill-forts and a whole host of villages.

Man has passed this way throughout the ages, as evidenced by these monuments by him, to him and for him. A building can be an azoic entity; a village is not.

And sometimes one just wishes that one could—as an old Cotsaller suggested an irate lady should, who jealously guarded the strip of road which was her private right of way: "if it means that much to thee, thee ought to be able to roll it up and kip it under thy bed".

Index